HISTORIC AIRCRAFT AND SPACECRAFT

IN THE
CRADLE OF AVIATION MUSEUM

JOSHUA STOFF

DOVER PUBLICATIONS, INC.
MINEOLA, NEW YORK

Frontispiece: A Grumman F-11 in the Cradle of Aviation Museum.

~

Copyright

Copyright © 2001 by Nassau Heritage
All rights reserved under Pan American and International Copyright Conventions.

Published in Canada by General Publishing Company, Ltd., 895 Don Mills Road, 400-2 Park Centre, Toronto, Ontario M3C 1W3.
Published in the United Kingdom by David & Charles, Brunel House, Forde Close, Newton Abbot, Devon TQ12 4PU.

Bibliographical Note

Historic Aircraft and Spacecraft in the Cradle of Aviation Museum is a publication of Nassau Heritage and the Cradle of Aviation Museum, Garden City, N.Y. This is a new work, first published by Dover Publications in 2001.

Library of Congress Cataloging-in-Publication Data

Stoff, Joshua.
    Historic aircraft and spacecraft in the Cradle of Aviation Museum / Joshua Stoff.
        p. cm.
    Includes index.
    ISBN 0-486-42041-8 (pbk.)
    1. Cradle of Aviation Museum. 2. Aeronautics—Museums—New York—Garden City. 3. Astronautics—Museums—New York—Garden City. 4. Airplanes—History—Sources. 5. Space vehicles—History—Sources.

TL506.U52 G377 2001
629.13'0074'747245—dc21

                                                                        2001047568

Book design by Carol Belanger Grafton

Manufactured in the United States of America
Dover Publications, Inc., 31 East 2nd Street, Mineola, N.Y. 11501

Table of Contents

Foreword

The Cradle of Aviation Museum air and space collection had its beginnings with the establishment of the Nassau County Historical Museum in the late 1950s. A small collection of aviation artifacts, along with archival and library materials, was housed in the museum when it opened in Eisenhower Park, East Meadow, in 1961.

To those concerned with the preservation of our aviation heritage, however, this arrangement came to seem insufficient. In 1969, I joined with museum supporter Preston Bassett, former president of Sperry Gyroscope (and author of an article, "Long Island, Cradle of Aviation") to propose that a new museum with a major air and space collection be included in the planned Kennedy Cultural Center at the former Mitchel Air Field, which had recently been acquired by the county. County Executive Eugene Nickerson agreed, as did his successor Ralph Caso, who in the early 1970s included the proposal in plans for a Bicentennial Center with a new 100,000-square-foot county museum.

Subsequently, the Nassau County Museum became a division of the County Department of Recreation and Parks. William K. Kaiser, a former naval aviator and educator, joined the staff and through the 1970s developed its volunteer program while expanding its air and space collections. A citizens' group, the Friends for Long Island's Heritage, provided support for the museum's programs, including the future air and space installations. Extensive local support and liaison with the military and the National Air and Space Museum was developed (and continues to the present day). An original sister ship of the *Spirit of St. Louis* was purchased in 1976 and Charles Lindbergh's Jenny was acquired by Friends trustee George Dade, a major future supporter of the collections program.

Although the Bicentennial Center was eventually deleted from the county budget, the aviation concept remained part of the county museum program. In 1979 two of the remaining Mitchel Field hangars became a warehouse and restoration center for air and space collections. Subsequently, under curator Joshua Stoff's leadership, an aggressive effort established the present significant collection. A dedicated, skilled volunteer force has made possible the highest standard of air and spacecraft restoration and replication.

In 1980 the first of a series of county capital funds grants enabled plans for a major air and space museum, including an Imax theater. Despite changes in the county administration, both executive and legislative branches supported this master plan; funding by 1997 totaled over $40,000,000 for construction, an amount matched by citizen contributions for acquisition and restoration.

The Cradle of Aviation Museum, the Leroy R. and Rose W. Grumman Imax Dome Theater, and the Reckson Center today provide over 130,000 square feet of museum space dedicated to the spirit of discovery and to Long Island's leading role in American achievements in air and space technology. Their world-class collection and building provide an active interpretation program for visitors and are the major components of the Museums at Mitchel, a complex of facilities managed and operated by Nassau Heritage, an educational corporation chartered by the State of New York. They will be the major resources for a future Aerospace Adventure Program—one that will give hands-on experience to members of new generations as they prepare for the challenges of new frontiers in aviation and outer space.

EDWARD J. SMITS
CEO, Nassau Heritage

Introduction

The Apollo 15 moon landing, July 30, 1971.

To fly like the birds has always been a dream of mankind. Indeed, the very idea of flight has always intrigued us. Today, even though we are accustomed to soaring through the sky in a Boeing 747 (for only the price of a ticket!), the idea of so enormous an object rising from the ground and flying under its own power can still strike us with awe. Awe of this kind inspired countless attempts over the centuries to emulate the birds. Every one of these attempts ended in dismal failure—until December 17, 1903.

On that day, Orville Wright's amazing flight over the sand dunes near Kitty Hawk, North Carolina, seemed to break an age-old spell that had prevented man from conquering the air. Quickly, scientists, tinkerers, daredevils, inventors and mechanics all plunged headlong into the great adventure. Now triumph was followed by triumph—and often by spectacular failure. For modern achievements in aviation did not come without great cost, and both lives and fortunes were lost.

Today, when flying around the world is safer than driving to a nearby grocery, it is hard to keep in mind how dangerous flying was in those early days. For the first thirty years or so, nearly all airplanes were fragile wooden structures braced by wires and covered with varnished fabric. Even the safest of those pioneering planes were, relative to today's, deathtraps. To leave the safety of Mother Earth on those frail wings and climb into the sky, which the pioneers of flight knew they were penetrating only at great risk, demanded a unique blend of courage, dedication, curiosity and fanaticism. And amazingly, within less than seventy years of the Wrights' first flight—the span of a single lifetime—new pioneers had walked upon the moon.

Over the course of 80 years, aviation grew up on, boomed on, and helped shape Long Island. Long Island has without doubt helped transform aviation from a dangerous sport to a viable means of commercial transportation. Long Islanders have also produced a large portion of the nation's aerial arsenal in time of war. The contributions by Long Islanders and Long Island corporations to the development of aviation and spaceflight, and their key roles in making aviation central to our world today, are the central focus of the Cradle of Aviation Museum.

Strategically placed economically, Long Island is also geographically well suited to have served the development of aviation. Located at the eastern edge of the United States, on the Atlantic Ocean and adjacent to America's most populous city, it is an ideal focal point for transatlantic and transcontinental flights. The central area of Nassau County, known as the Hempstead Plains, is the only natural prairie east of the Allegheny Mountains. Treeless and flat, with only tall grasses and scattered farmhouses, this area proved to be an ideal flying field, and was the scene of intense aviation activity for over 50 years.

Although Long Island has long been known as "The Cradle of American Aviation," it has also had a very long involvement with the American space program. After hundreds of thousands of years of occupancy, and several thousand years of recorded history, man at last left the planet Earth in the twentieth century and took the first hesitant steps on a world that was not his own. Long Islanders made these first steps possible. Long Island's involvement with spaceflight can be traced back to Robert Goddard's earliest, pioneering experiments in rocketry, and it continues through the development of the lunar module, the international space station and beyond. In all, a vast amount of historic aerospace activity has taken place on Long Island (more than 64,000 aircraft have been built here)—remarkable in view of the fact that Long Island is really not such a large place.

Today, Long Islanders see more air traffic going over their heads than any other people on earth, although today's

The remains of a CG-4A glider, as found in Pennsylvania in 1989. Restored by the museum, it is one of only four survivors of the over 14,000 built during World War II.

The museum's P-84B Thunderjet in Death Valley prior to restoration. Built in 1947, this plane is the oldest surviving Long Island-built production jet.

The museum's F4F-3 Wildcat during recovery from Lake Michigan in 1989. It had crashed during a training flight in 1944.

The museum's Grumman Agcat under restoration in 2001.

Charles Lindbergh (l) and George Dade examine the remains of Lindbergh's Jenny, now in the museum, at Dade's Glen Head home, 1974.

Museum staff picking up rare floats for the Curtiss Robin in New Hampshire.

Boeing 747s and SSTs do not turn nearly as many heads as did Glenn Curtiss' tiny biplane in 1909. Aviation is taken for granted now, but it has shaped our lives to a degree greater than we can imagine.

To preserve this heritage for future generations, Nassau County has undertaken the development of a major air and space museum. Located at historic Mitchel Field, the museum's primary mission is to collect, preserve and interpret the aerospace heritage of Long Island. Thus some 65 historic aircraft and spacecraft have been procured for the museum, most of them built on Long Island and each directly relevant to Long Island's aerospace heritage. These craft have been obtained through private and corporate donation, government loan, or purchase by the museum's support organization, The Friends for Long Island's Heritage. The vast majority have been painstakingly and meticulously restored by the museum's skilled volunteer corps, which consists mostly of retirees from the aerospace industry.

For over twenty years an extensive worldwide search has been conducted to locate aircraft and spacecraft associated with or built on Long Island. This search has taken museum staff from the bottom of Lake Michigan to the woods of Pennsylvania and the deserts of California, across the seas to Turkey and Russia and the far-off shores of Guadalcanal, and it has created one of the world's outstanding and most diverse collections. Many of the historic aircraft are very rare; eleven are the only surviving representatives of their type. This unequaled collection is one of the few in the world incorporating both military and civilian aircraft and spacecraft, and it represents all key periods in aerospace history. It is a priceless national treasure—although it will never really be complete.

The history of aviation, of course, is more than just the history of hardware. The aircraft and spacecraft in the museum's collection, which took us from the Hempstead Plains to the moon, were actually designed, built and flown by our parents, our grandparents, our siblings, our neighbors and perhaps even ourselves. Our aerospace history is important because our heritage, carried from one generation to another, enables us to know better who we are and where we are going. Our museum is educational, inspirational, heartlifting and heartbreaking. It gives a home to our memories, and they in turn connect us in some vital, intangible, and very personal way to our yesterdays and our tomorrows. This is hands-on history; it is what our fathers and mothers did, and it explains in part who we may be because it tells us the way we were. All the joy and pathos, the horror and hope, of the human condition can be found here. That yesterday was—we know for certain. That tomorrow might be—we can only hope. Tying one to the other is what our museum does, and those connections make the museum a very enriching and unique experience.

The eight permanent galleries in the Cradle of Aviation Museum provide a walkway through time that traces the development of American aviation as seen through a Long Island lens, beginning with nineteenth-century ballooning and moving forward to present-day space exploration. Dioramic full-scale recreations of a 1910 Hempstead Plains air meet, a World War II aircraft carrier flight deck and the lunar module landing on the Moon, among others, present visitors with a you-are-there view of historic events and the role Long Island played in them. Altogether the visual effect of each gallery is quite spectacular. We have chosen a different approach from other museums in the world, combining historical artifacts and graphic material with emotional impressions, focusing not so much on the aircraft as on the people and ideas behind them. Each gallery also provides a personal focus by portraying the pivotal Long Island achievements of individuals—not just the heroic pilots such as Charles Lindbergh andothers less well known, but also the expert and dedicated individuals who designed and built their air and spacecraft.

The aircraft, spacecraft and other artifacts and exhibits in the Cradle of Aviation Museum attest that, from the earliest days of aviation, Long Islanders have been leaders as flyers, designers and builders of air and space craft. Thus it is appropriate that Long Island now has one of the best air and space museums in the world. Aviation and space flight are very special to Long Island and they have touched many of our lives. At long last, we have a place to preserve and enjoy this important part of our history.

JOSHUA STOFF
Curator

Early Aeronautica

A nineteenth-century drawing of the basket for a gas balloon.

A nineteenth-century gas balloon.

BALLOON BASKET, 1880 (replica)

The earliest form of flight by man was ballooning, a pioneering form of air travel that never became very popular on Long Island. After all, the Island is a relatively small body of land surrounded by saltwater, and early balloonists had no desire to get blown out to sea! The first balloon to land on Long Island had lifted off from New York City. The year was 1833, just 50 years after the Montgolfier brothers had made their historic first flight in a hot air ballooon. Several more flights on Long Island were recorded in the 1860s and 70s. The most famous occurred in 1873, when W. H. Donaldson and a crew of two attempted a transatlantic flight in a huge gas balloon. The flight took off from Brooklyn and proceeded east and north across Long Island Sound. But a violent storm blew up over Connecticut, and the men were forced to jump out to safety. Thus the first transatlantic flight from Long Island lasted only 60 miles.

The envelope of a gas balloon in the nineteenth century was usually made of woven fabric, coated with varnish in order to increase its resistance to rips and to slow the escape of gas. A rope netting covering the envelope uniformly distributed the weight of the basket, which hung from a suspension hoop. The balloon was inflated with hydrogen or coal gas through an opening at its bottom. Once released, the aircraft ascended until its weight was in equilibrium with the air around it. Sand ballast was dropped to make the balloon rise higher, and gas was released through a valve to cause it to descend.

The wicker balloon basket on display dates from the 1950s and was modified to resemble a nineteenth-century balloon basket.

1

Oscar Freymann with a model of his ornithopter.

FREYMANN ORNITHOPTER, 1896

Man's earliest (and always unsuccessful) heavier-than-air attempts to fly were in ornithopters—devices with flapping wings that were a mechanical imitation of bird flight. Would-be aviators reasoned that if birds could fly by flapping their wings, then why couldn't people do the same thing? They were wrong. Ornithopters proved to be far too heavy, cumbersome, and underpowered to generate sufficient lift. Nevertheless, inventors like Oscar Freymann refused to give up. As a youth living in Russia, Freymann had observed eagles in flight and determined to build a flying machine based on the actions he saw. After emigrating to America in 1895 he worked in a bicycle shop in Brooklyn. (At the same time Wilbur and Orville Wright were working in their bike shop in Dayton, Ohio.) Freymann soon built his flying machine, with four wings operated by the pedaling action of a bicycle. Moving the handle bars turned a rudder at the rear. In November 1896, Freymann and three other men trucked the machine to an open field in the town of Flatbush. He claims to have pedaled furiously and flown the ornithopter to an altitude of 14 feet—but this is quite doubtful. In any event the machine was damaged during the trial and never rebuilt. Freymann ultimately planned on building a larger, gasoline-powered ornithopter on a tricycle, but he ran out of money and abandoned the project.

The model on display was also built by Freymann in the 1890s, to help him work out the wing-flapping system.

TIMMONS KITE, 1906

Kites are basically tethered heavier-than-air craft that derive their lift solely from the wind. In the nineteenth and early twentieth centuries building and flying kites was popular with many enthusiasts on Long Island. One of the most interesting home-built kites was made by young Nicholas Timmons of South Ozone Park, Queens, in 1906. He may have modeled his tandem biplane kite after a Langley design (see page 7). The Timmons model on display attracted considerable attention when it was flown. The propellers were unpowered and merely turned in the breeze for effect.

The Timmons kite.

Historic Kite Designs

Most of us at some point have attempted to fly a kite. It is generally believed that the kite was invented in China about 3000 years ago, but its history remains obscure.

The uses of the kite have been many and varied, and it has undoubtedly contributed to the desire to extend human physical and mental reach. Undoubtedly though, the kite's greatest contribution has been its role as a precursor of the airplane. In fact, many early aviation pioneers based their designs upon successful kite applications. These historic kite designs can be seen in the first gallery at the Cradle of Aviation Museum.

EDDY KITE

William Eddy, a journalist from Bayonne, New Jersey, contributed a great deal to western kite development and made extensive experiments in the raising of photographic and meteorological payloads. In the 1890s, Eddy developed an efficient, stable, cruciform kite that could be flown without a tail. By using a flexible spar, the kite would bow in the wind, thus acting like a ship's keel in water. The loose cover would also billow upwards, acting to some extent as an airfoil, giving additional lift.

HARGRAVE KITE

Lawrence Hargrave was an Englishman who migrated to Australia in 1866. His experiments with kites were a byproduct of his ambition to achieve powered flight. He invented the box kite in 1893, and his kite experiments using a cambered airfoil for greater lift were a major contribution to aerodynamics. In order to further his experiments in powered flight, which were ultimately unsuccessful, he built a great variety of model airplanes and kites in the 1890s.

William Eddy with one of his kites.

Getting ready to fly a Hargrave kite.

BADEN-POWELL KITE

A pioneer of the heavy-lift kite was B. F. S. Baden-Powell, brother of the founder of the Boy Scouts. In the 1890s he developed the large hexagonal "Levitor" or "Manlifter" kite for the British army. It was designed to lift a man for aerial observation. In 1901 radio pioneer Guglielmo Marconi made the first successful transatlantic wireless (radio) tests by raising an antenna 400 feet by means of a Baden-Powell Levitor kite.

CODY KITE

One of the most flamboyant early aviation pioneers was the American expatriate Samuel F. Cody. A wild west showman (like his hero William F. "Buffalo Bill" Cody, whose name he took as his own), Cody settled in England in 1890. In 1900 he became interested in aeronautics and he soon developed a large winged box kite for man-lifting experiments. The British War Office carried out extensive trials in 1904 and adopted the system for aerial observation in 1906. Cody's courage and enthusiasm further led him to experiment with powered flight and in 1908 he became the first man to build and fly an airplane in Britain.

A Baden-Powell kite as used by Marconi.

Samuel F. Cody (on horseback) with his kite, as one of his men stands in the basket, preparing to lift off.

4

The Bell tetrahedral kite.

BELL KITE

Scots-Canadian Alexander Graham Bell, inventor of the telephone, also experimented with aeronautics beginning in the 1890s. While living in Nova Scotia, Bell embarked on a remarkable program of kite tests directed towards establishing the most stable form of kite capable of carrying a man and an engine. Bell eventually decided upon the tetrahedral cell kite, a structure found to possess great lift as well as strength. In 1907, a tetrahedral kite made up of over 3000 cells lifted a man to almost 200 feet while towed behind a boat. However, a powered version of the kite was found to be incapable of developing sufficient thrust to overcome the massive drag. Nonetheless, Bell's kite experimentation led him to other more conventional designs which eventually resulted in a successful powered aircraft.

LILIENTHAL KITE (replica)

For some years Otto Lilienthal of Germany had been interested in human flight. He attempted to unlock the secrets of birds by studying the wings of the albatross (a wandering albatross can have a wingspread of 11 feet). In 1874 Lilienthal unveiled his flying machine, a kite with a wing shape (an airfoil) to help it gain lift. His success with this kite led him to build his famous man-carrying gliders.

WRIGHT KITE (replica)

Before their first experiments with gliders, Orville and Wilbur Wright built and flew this kite in a field near their home in Dayton, Ohio. The year was 1899. From this, their first flying machine, the Wrights worked out their novel idea for wing warping—that is, twisting the wings to turn the machine. The successful flights of their kite inspired the Wrights to continue their intense study of possible methods of human flight.

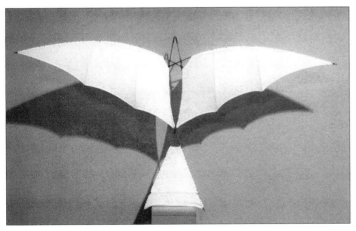

The Lilienthal kite.

The Wright kite.

Lilienthal Glider

GERMANY, 1894 (replica)

Augustus Herring of Freeport with Lilienthal-type glider, ca. 1895.

The daring pioneers who built and flew manned gliders near the end of the nineteenth century laid the foundation for the design of the first successful flying machines. Otto Lilienthal, a German born in 1848, was the most important member of this group. At the age of twenty-three he began to conduct serious research in aeronautics. Not content to work in theory alone, he developed a series of gliders that he hoped would demonstrate the feasibility of manned flight. By 1894 Lilienthal had built what he considered his safest and most successful flying machine, a glider made of a willow frame covered with cotton cloth. The wings were designed to fold to the rear for transportation and storage. As in all Lilienthal gliders, the pilot was suspended between the wings on bars attached to the frame. Movement of the pilot's body altered the center of gravity and provided the only form of control. Taking off from a 100-foot hill, Lilienthal made many flights of up to 1,150 feet in gliders of this type, effectively demonstrating that the air could support a man in winged flight.

In 1896, American newspaper publisher William Randolph Hearst, then living in Sands Point, purchased a Lilienthal glider, the only American to do so. Hearst felt that public interest in flying would help to sell his newspaper, the New York *Journal*, and saw to it that the *Journal* carried stories of its test flights. Hearst's glider flew in the spring of 1896, perhaps on Long Island, where it would have been the first heavier-than-air craft to do so. Also on Long Island, Freeport resident and aeronautical pioneer Augustus Herring built a Lilienthal-type glider in 1894. He flew it in northern Manhattan in 1895 and, with aviation pioneer Octave Chanute, in Michigan in 1896. Hearst called off his tests after Lilienthal died in a glider crash in Germany on August 10, 1896. Although his aeronautical experiments thus came to a premature halt, Lilienthal's work exerted a tremendous influence on the progress of manned flight in the United States.

The aircraft on display is a full-scale exact replica of Lilienthal's 1894 glider, constructed by skilled museum volunteers working from original plans.

Specifications

Wingspan: 26'
Length: 13'1"
Top speed: about 20 MPH

Otto Lilienthal, flying his glider, 1896.

Langley Aerodrome No. 5

WASHINGTON, D.C., 1895 (replica)

The Langley Aerodrome in flight.

Professor Samuel P. Langley (1834–1906), astronomer and, after 1887, Secretary of the Smithsonian Institution, was one of the first major aeronautical figures in the United States. Prior to joining the Smithsonian he had conducted theoretical investigations of aerodynamics, including some experiments with rubber band-powered models.

In 1891 he embarked on practical experiments with large, tandem-winged models powered by steam and gasoline engines, and on May 6, 1896, his Aerodrome No. 5 made the first successful flight of any powered heavier-than-air flying machine. It was launched from a catapult mounted on top of a houseboat on the Potomac River not far from Washington. Two flights were made on May 6, one of 3,300 feet and one of 2,500 feet, and on both flights the aircraft climbed and turned with ease. It landed in the water, as planned; in order to save weight, it was not equipped with landing gear.

The powerplant of Aerodrome No. 5 consisted of a single-cylinder steam engine and a flash-tube boiler fired by a gasoline burner. The engine drove two propellers through a system of shafts and bevel gears. The aircraft's wood and steel-tube frame was covered with silk. In 1903 Langley attempted to fly a much larger, man-carrying, Aerodrome built along the same lines as No. 5, but it failed on two occasions because of problems with the launching mechanism. The two most important engineers in Langley's aeronautical experimentation were Charles Manly and Augustus Herring, both residents of Freeport, Long Island.

The aircraft on display is a full-scale replica of Aerodrome No. 5, built from original plans by museum volunteers.

Specifications

Wingspan: 13'8"
Length: 13'2"
Engine: Langley steam engine, 1 HP
Top speed: 25 MPH
Weight: 30 lbs

Blériot Type XI

FRANCE, 1909

The Blériot Type XI was the most famous and successful of the several classic aircraft that first appeared in the summer of 1909. It was developed in France by Louis Blériot, who had made a fortune in the early automobile industry before becoming an aviation pioneer. Blériot and his aircraft achieved immortality on July 25, 1909, by making the first air crossing of the English Channel. They covered the 24 miles between Calais and Dover in 36 minutes. Although underpowered and unstable (like all pre-World War I aircraft), the Type XI became quite popular. It was not long before enterprising U.S. manufacturers began to build and sell copies of it.

On Long Island, Blériots were built by the American Aeroplane Supply House (AASH) in Hempstead. This was the first of many aircraft manufacturing companies to operate on Long Island. Between 1911 and 1913 four basic models were produced, costing between $2,700 and $6,000, depending on the type of engine. During 1911 AASH sold more Blériots than all other U.S. manufacturers combined. However, in all, it produced only about fifteen aircraft and ceased operation in 1914. Also on Long Island, the Moisant Flying School, founded in Mineola in 1911 and one of the first in the U.S., operated seven Blériot monoplanes. In fact, the first licensed American woman pilot, Harriet Quimby, learned to fly on a Blériot at the Moisant School. This aircraft is of the same type that was flown by Earle Ovington when he made the first official American Air Mail flights, at the Nassau Boulevard International Air Meet, between September 23 and October 1, 1911. These flights, from Garden City to Mineola, covered a distance of six miles.

The aircraft on display, serial no. 153, was purchased for the museum from the Old Rhinebeck Aerodrome by the Friends for Long Island's Heritage, sponsored by Alan Fortunoff. The Blériot is perhaps the most prized plane in the museum's collection. It is the fourth-oldest aircraft in the United States, and quite possibly among the ten oldest in the world. It was built at the Blériot factory near Paris and was purchased for $2,200 by Rodman Wanamaker, a wealthy American merchant. Arriving in New York in November 1909, it was the first aircraft to be imported into the United States. Wanamaker promptly resold it for $5,000 to another wealthy aviation enthusiast, Louis Bergdoll. It is quite possible that this airplane was flown over Long Island in 1910–11. In any case, the Blériot Type XI was the most common aircraft on Long Island before World War I.

Specifications

Wingspan: 28'6"
Length: 25'5"
Top speed: 45 MPH
Engine: 30 HP Anzani
Weight: 620 lbs

An early advertisement for the Long Island-built Blériot.

Louis Bergdoll, standing by his Type XI airplane.

Herring-Curtiss Golden Flyer

HAMMONDSPORT, NEW YORK, 1909 (replica)

Long Island's first successful powered flights of a heavier-than-air craft were made by the Herring-Curtiss *Golden Flyer* in July 1909 on the Hempstead Plains next to the Mineola Fairgrounds. In these first flights, the aviation industry on Long Island was born.

Famed aeronautical pioneer Glenn Curtiss had made the first public demonstration flight of an airplane in America in 1908, and he was subsequently commissioned (for $5,000) by the New York Aeronautic Society to provide an aircraft for their use. The Aeronautic Society had been founded in 1908 by a group of gentlemen interested in aviation, many of them aspiring to become pilots. The group had been operating out of the Morris Park Racetrack in the Bronx, but its small confines led to the suggestion that Curtiss demonstrate the *Golden Flyer* (so called because of the color of its fabric covering) on the open expanses of Long Island's Hempstead Plains. After surveying the environs of Mineola, Curtiss readily assented to move there in May 1909. The new flying field proved to be ideal, with an almost complete absence of trees. It was level and well-drained, had no smokestacks or other obstacles, and provided a long, open sweep with plenty of room for maneuvering. Besides offering flight instruction to the members of the Aeronautic Society, Curtiss practiced in the *Golden Flyer* for the first great International Aviation Tournament at Rheims, France.

The Herring-Curtiss Company was founded in upstate Hammondsport, New York by Curtiss and Freeport resident and gliding pioneer Augustus Herring, who raised the balance of the capital. Although the company existed for only a short time, it was the first manufacturer in the United States to build, advertise, sell, and deliver an airplane. The *Golden Flyer* was constructed of spruce and bamboo with rubberized silk covering. For its day it proved to be strong, fairly fast, and highly manageable. This last trait was the result of an innovation: installing ailerons between the wings. The pilot operated the ailerons by leaning to the side against the movable bars around his seat. On July 16, 1909, Curtiss flew the *Golden Flyer* from Mineola on a flight officially exceeding 25 kilometers and won the *Scientific American* Trophy for the first airplane flight of this length in America.

The museum's exact replica of the *Golden Flyer* was constructed by volunteers from original plans and represents the type of American aircraft that gained the most popularity in America in the years prior to World War I. The original *Golden Flyer* crashed and was destroyed in 1910.

Specifications

Wingspan: 28'9"
Length: 30'4"
Engine: 25 HP 4-cylinder Curtiss
Top speed: 45 MPH
Weight: 550 lbs

Glen Curtiss (second from right) and crew with the *Golden Flyer* at Mineola.

Wright Model B Vin Fiz

DAYTON, OHIO, 1911 (replica)

Hats off as Cal Rogers takes off from Sheepshead Bay in the *Vin Fiz*.

On September 17, 1911, Calbraith P. Rogers departed Sheepshead Bay, Brooklyn, in an attempt to win the $50,000 prize for the first transcontinental flight made in thirty days or less. The prize was announced by William Randolph Hearst in 1910 and was to expire on October 31, 1911.

Rogers's sponsor, the Armour Company of Chicago, was promoting a new carbonated grape drink named "Vin Fiz"; his aircraft, a Wright Model B, was emblazoned with the product's trademark. To provide repair facilities and assistance, a specially equipped service train followed him across the country. Rogers navigated the continent by simply following railroad tracks. His flight required seventy landings for service stops and was interrupted by no fewer than fifteen crashes. The difficulties of the flight were staggering: there were no airfields, no regular supplies, no weather reports, no instruments, and no flight plans. The mechanics on the train that followed the plane's route were never idle: landings were rarely made without damage, engine parts regularly gave out, and the stresses of bad weather took their toll—as did souvenir hunters.

Finally, on November 5, 1911, Rogers reached Pasadena, California, after traveling forty-nine days and 4,321 miles. His total flying time was eighty-two hours. Though he failed to win the prize, Rogers's perseverance and determination won him the admiration and support of the American public. The flight also showed the potential of the airplane. Sadly, barely four months after the flight, Rogers was killed in the crash of another Wright Model B.

The *Vin Fiz* on display is a full-scale replica built by museum volunteers from original plans. Complete with a modified Ford Model T engine, the aircraft is capable of flight.

Specifications

Wingspan: 31'6"
Length: 21'5"
Engine: 35 HP 4-cylinder Wright
Top speed: 55 MPH
Weight: 703 lbs

Curtiss JN-4 Jenny

BUFFALO, NEW YORK, 1918

The first Jenny, America's most famous airplane in World War I, was designed in 1914 and built by the Curtiss Aeroplane Company. The next year Curtiss produced the JN-3, combining the best features of its J and N models. Its poor performance in the U.S. Army's 1916 expedition against Pancho Villa in Mexico brought about important modifications, and by 1917 the famous JN-4 was in full production. Powered by a water-cooled Curtiss OX-5 engine, with a framework of ash covered in cotton fabric, the new Jenny cruised at 45 MPH. Its main function was as a primary flight trainer for the Army Air Service, but some Jennys were also equipped with machine guns and bombs for advanced training. In 1917 and 1918 the JN-4 was used extensively on Long Island for flight training at Hazelhurst, Mitchel, and Brindley fields. By the time the Armistice was signed, about 6,000 Jennys had been delivered to the Army. Production ceased, but soon the civil aviation market was filled with hundreds of surplus Jenny for sale at prices as low as $50 each. Many of the pilots who bought them flew around the countryside in the 1920s, landing in open fields or farms, where they put on air shows and offered rides for a price. These men who first brought aviation to the general public were called "barnstormers."

The Jenny on display was purchased in 1923 by the 21-year-old Charles Lindbergh in Americus, Georgia, for $500. It was the first aircraft he ever owned. During the next two years, before joining the Air Service (without a pilot's license—they were not required until 1926), Lindbergh barnstormed with the plane throughout the Midwest. He survived two minor crashes, repairing most of the resulting damage himself. The plane ended its flying days in a crash after Lindbergh sold it, and came to rest in a pig barn in Coggin, Iowa.

George Dade, an aviation enthusiast on Long Island, located the plane, purchased it, and had it restored by members of the Long Island Early Fliers Club between 1973 and 1976. It was the first airplane the museum acquired. Charles Lindbergh came to view the restoration in progress just months before his death and, peering beneath all the modifications and repairs, verified that it was indeed his old Jenny. It is displayed configured as Lindbergh flew it in 1923. In addition, the museum possesses a JN-4 fuselage, with both original and reproduction parts, displayed uncovered so visitors can examine its construction.

This airplane is on permanent loan from the Long Island Early Fliers Club.

Specifications

Wingspan: 43'7"
Length: 27'4"
Engine: 90 HP Curtiss OX-5
Top speed: 75 MPH
Weight: 1,430 lbs

Barnstormers Leon Klink and Charles Lindbergh (right) pose in front of their JN-4D Jenny.

An unidentified pilot in front of a Jenny at Mitchel Field, 1918.

Breese Penguin

A flight line of Breese Penguins, 1918.

During World War I France exerted a tremendous influence on the organization of the military aviation program in the United States. One of the recommendations the French made was the development of a nonflying trainer that would give student pilots the feel of airplane controls at near-flying speeds on the ground. Only one model of this type, the Penguin, was produced. In late 1917 the Breese Aircraft Corporation of Farmingdale received a U.S. government contract to deliver 300 Penguins. These planes were designed along the lines of a French Blériot, but their wings were too short and their engines too small to allow them to fly. They were equipped with small two-cylinder engines built by the Lawrance Engine Corporation, also of Farmingdale.

The Penguins had no brakes or steerable wheels, making them quite difficult to control. They were intended for use in the transition between the slow primary training models and the high-speed military types, whose handling characteristics during takeoff and landing were difficult to master. Penguins were intended to be just as unmanageable and thus give trainee pilots some experience in the difficulties of controlling airplanes moving at high speeds. Breese completed its order for all 300 Penguins by the fall of 1918. The planes were retained in use until at least May of 1920, when they were taken out of service and condemned to be scrapped.

The Breese Penguin on display is the only one known to be still in existence. Remarkably, it retains its original 1918 fabric and finish. The machine was purchased for the museum from the Wings and Wheels Collection in Florida by the Friends for Long Island's Heritage.

Specifications

Wingspan: 14'4"
Length: 19'2"
Top speed: 35 MPH
Engine: 28 HP Lawrance
Weight: 690 lbs

Thomas-Morse S4C Scout

ITHACA, NEW YORK, 1918

The Thomas-Morse Scout was the best fighter training airplane produced in the U.S. during World War I. Dubbed the "Tommy" by the pilots who flew it, the plane had a long and varied career. It first appeared in the summer of 1917 as the S4B, 100 of which were ordered. A slightly modified version, the S4C, was later developed and 497 were purchased by the Air Service. Equipped with an 80 HP LeRhone rotary engine, the Thomas-Morse is essentially an American copy of the British Sopwith Pup. The rotary engine, peculiar to World War I planes, is unique in that in order to cool the engine properly, the entire engine had to revolve with the propeller. The crankshaft is thus bolted to the plane, with the engine and propeller rotating around it.

Tommys were used at practically every pursuit flying school in the U.S. during 1918, including Mitchel Field. Mitchel Field was named after former New York City Mayor John Purroy Mitchel, who was killed flying a Scout during Air Service training in 1918. After the war ended, many were sold as surplus to civilian flying schools, sportsman pilots and ex-Army fliers.

The aircraft on display is one of only ten surviving examples of the over 500 Scouts built. It has been based on Long Island continuously since being purchased as surplus at Mitchel Field in 1923. It was based at Roosevelt Field through World War II, and later at Fitzmaurice Field in Massapequa. From the 1920s through the 1950s, Paul Kotze of Merrick barnstormed the metropolitan area, performing at many air shows and festivals. Equipped with its original Marlin machine gun, the plane is one of the best preserved World War I fighters and is still airworthy.

On permanent loan from Mr. Paul Kotze.

Specifications

Wingspan: 26'6"
Length: 19'10"
Engine: 90 HP LeRhone
Top speed: 95 MPH
Weight: 1,330 lbs

A Thomas-Morse Scout at Mitchel Field, 1919.

Curtiss/Sperry Aerial Torpedo

GARDEN CITY, 1918 (replica)

A Curtiss/Sperry Aerial Torpedo on the rails, ready to go.

The Sperry Aerial Torpedo program (1917–18) was the first "guided missile" program carried on in this country, if not in the world. The Sperry Company of Brooklyn had developed automatic control devices for aircraft as early as 1913. In 1916 Lawrence Sperry, son of the inventor Elmer Sperry, formed a new company and moved his autopilot operations to a more isolated site at Amityville on the Great South Bay. The U.S. Navy soon became interested in the project and agreed to fund the development of unmanned aircraft to be used as "aerial torpedoes" or "flying bombs." These were designed to be launched under their own power; after a predetermined period the engine would cut off, and the torpedo would dive into its target.

Five small Aerial Torpedoes were built by the Curtiss Company at Garden City. At first, efforts were made to launch them from a hanging cable, but these failed. Lawrence Sperry resorted to modifying and flying the Aerial Torpedo himself in an effort to prove its airworthiness. Soon a special track dolly and catapult were developed, and this system met with some success.

With the end of World War I, all experiments with unmanned flying bombs came to a halt. Nonetheless, the successful Aerial Torpedo flight of March 16, 1918, from Amityville, marked the first time a full-size, automatically controlled unmanned aircraft had actually flown. Furthermore, improvements in the Aerial Torpedoes' gyroscopes were reflected in Sperry's automatic pilots of later years. In effect, Sperry's Aerial Torpedo is a direct ancestor of the modern cruise missile.

The aircraft on display is a full-scale replica of the Curtiss/Sperry Aerial Torpedo. It was built by museum volunteers, who incorporated an original 1918 Curtiss OX-5 engine.

Specifications

Wingspan: 22'
Length: 15'
Engine: 90 HP Curtiss OX-5
Top speed: 70 MPH
Weight: 950 lbs

A high-speed test of an Aerial Torpedo atop a Marmon automobile.

Aircraft Engineering Corporation Ace

CENTRAL PARK (BETHPAGE), 1918

The diminutive Ace was the first American sport airplane to be commercially produced for the civilian market following World War I. Built very much along the lines of a wartime fighter plane, the aircraft was hailed as "America's premier sport plane." It was partially built in New York City, but all finishing, final assembly, and flight testing took place at Central Park (Bethpage) Flying Field. The four-cylinder, water-cooled engine was built in North Beach, Queens. The Ace was quite a performer for its day, taking off within 80 feet, climbing to 2,500 feet in eight minutes, and landing in only 60 feet of runway. Priced at $2,500, roughly the cost of an average house on Long Island at the time, the aircraft was also capable of impressive aerobatics. The chief test pilot of the Ace was Bruce Eytinge, a former RAF flight instructor. Eddie Stinson, an Air Corps ace who went on to found the aircraft company bearing his name, was involved in promoting the plane.

Unfortunately, the Ace was a commercial failure. It appears that only seven were built. A major problem was the large number of surplus World War I Jennys on the postwar market. Without this competition the Ace might have seen widespread use as a light, economical aircraft with a low-horsepower engine.

The aircraft on display is the only Ace still in existence. It was originally delivered to Clifford Durant of Oakland, California, in 1919. On January 20, 1920, Air Corps pilot Lt. C. V. Pickup, flying it down an Oakland street as part of a shopping promotion, hit a utility pole and sheared a wing, ending the stunt. Remarkably, the plane was not scrapped but was stored in a garage loft, where it was discovered by Lorrill Lowery in 1952. Mr. Lowery spent the next three years restoring the aircraft, and on July 27, 1955, the Ace took to the air once again. This aircraft is now the second-oldest airworthy Long Island-built plane in the world. It was purchased for the museum from the Owl's Head (Maine) Transportation Museum by the Friends for Long Island's Heritage.

Specifications

Wingspan: 28' 4"
Length: 19' 2"
Top speed: 80 MPH
Engine: 40 HP Horace Keane Acemotor
Weight: 600 lbs

An advertisement for the Ace, *Flying* magazine, October 1919.

An Ace at Central Park flying field, 1919.

Sperry Messenger

FARMINGDALE, 1922 (replica)

In the years following World War I, the U. S. Air Service designed a number of its own airplanes and asked the aircraft industry to bid on contracts to build them. The Messenger was designed in 1920 at McCook Field, to provide the Army with a light message carrier intended to replace the motorcycle. Powered by a novel three-cylinder 64-hp Lawrance engine built on Long Island, the Messenger was designed as a practical single-seat airplane that would be able to fly out of small unprepared fields and from country roads.

The Lawrence Sperry Aircraft Company of Farmingdale won the contract and ultimately built 42 Messengers. Lawrence Sperry lived in Garden City and he kept the prototype Messenger for himself, using the road in front of his house as a runway. At one point he demonstrated his plane's capabilities by landing it on the plaza in front of the Capitol in Washington, D.C. In 1922 over Mitchel Field, Lawrence Sperry, using a Messenger, conducted the first experiments to test the feasibility of hooking an airplane onto an airship in flight. The next year he entered his aircraft in the St. Louis Air Races, placing fourth. In December 1923 Sperry was forced down in the English Channel and apparently drowned while trying to swim ashore.

The aircraft on display is a full-scale exact replica built by museum volunteers from original plans. Equipped with an engine based on the Lawrance, the aircraft is capable of flight.

Specifications

Wingspan: 20'
Length: 17' 9"
Top speed: 97 MPH
Engine: 64 HP Lawrance
Weight: 623 lbs

A Sperry Messenger in a Long Island field, 1922.

Lawrence Sperry, in a Messenger, takes off from a road near his home
in Garden City, 1922, followed by a motorcyle policeman.

Ryan Aircraft Brougham ("Spirit of St. Louis")

SAN DIEGO, CALIFORNIA, 1928

In 1919, Raymond Orteig, a wealthy hotel owner and aviation enthusiast, offered a prize of $25,000 for the first non-stop flight between New York and Paris. At the time, no aircraft was capable of such a flight. Early in 1927 a 25-year-old air mail pilot named Charles A. Lindbergh obtained the financial backing of a group of businessmen in St. Louis, Missouri to compete for the prize. In February of that year he placed an order with Ryan Aircraft of San Diego, California, for an airplane with specifications necessary for the flight. The aircraft was based on a Ryan M-2 mailplane, modified with a larger wing, a new and more powerful Wright J-5 engine, and a large fuel tank. The fuel tank was placed between engine and pilot, eliminating forward visibility so that the pilot's vision was restricted to side windows and a protruding periscope that provided a limited front view. The aircraft had a wooden wing and a steel-tube fuselage, both fabric-covered. Prior to Lindbergh's epic flight there had been several crashes and fatalities in unsuccessful attempts to fly between New York and Paris nonstop.

On the rainy morning of May 20, 1927, Lindbergh took off alone, heading for Paris. His muddy takeoff site was the original Roosevelt Field, just south of what is now The Source Mall on Old Country Road. After flying 3,610 miles in thirty-three hours and thirty minutes, he landed at LeBourget Airport, Paris, on time and on course, where he was greeted by a wildly enthusiastic crowd of over 100,000 people. Lindbergh and his heroic flight single-handedly revolutionized and popularized aviation as nothing before or since, and it clearly showed the future potential of commercial aviation. For the first time people seriously began to think of traveling by air.

The aircraft on display is an original sister ship of the *Spirit of St. Louis*. It was built in 1928 by Ryan as a "Brougham," an unsuccessful attempt to sell a commercial version of Lindy's famous airplane. One of only two surviving Broughams, it last flew on May 20, 1977, over Roosevelt Field on the fiftieth anniversary of Lindbergh's historic flight. Painted to look like the original *Spirit*, this aircraft was used in the 1955 movie *The Spirit of St. Louis*. It was purchased in Minnesota for the museum by the Friends for Long Island's Heritage.

Specifications

Wingspan: 46'
Length: 27'5
Engine: 220 HP Wright Whirlwind J-5-C
Top speed: 130 MPH
Weight: 2,150 lbs.

A formal portrait of the *Spirit of St. Louis*, taken in San Diego, California, 1927.

A small crowd gathers to watch as the *Spirit of St. Louis* is checked out
before takeoff, Roosevelt Field, May 20, 1927.

Brunner-Winkle Bird

GLENDALE, QUEENS, 1929

The Brunner-Winkle Aircraft Corporation was established in Glendale, Queens in 1928 by William Winkle, J. J. Finkle, and Joseph Brunner. The first airplane the company produced was the Model A Bird, powered by war-surplus Curtiss OX-5 engines. It was a three-seat open-cockpit plane designed by Michael Gregor. The forward cockpit could seat two persons side by side. The fuselage was made of steel tubing, and the wing frames were wooden. Both were covered with fabric. The Model A cruised at 80 MPH and sold for $3,150.

At the end of 1929 Brunner-Winkle introduced the Model B Bird, with the more powerful Kinner B-5 engine. The Bird also had two unique features not seen on other civilian aircraft of the period. It had a thick upper wing, which gave it high lift and allowed great control at low speeds. It also featured a radiator under the fuselage, giving it the appearance of a Curtiss Hawk fighter. Brunner-Winkle proved to be a short-lived firm, closing its doors in 1931 because of slow sales during the Depression.

Despite this commercial failure, the Bird itself was considered to be a fine airplane, the best of the OX-5-powered ships. In 1929 Elinor Smith set a new world endurance record for women when she flew a Bird for over thirteen hours over Roosevelt Field. In 1930 a Bird was entered in the Guggenheim Safe Plane Contest at Mitchel Field, where it performed admirably. Charles Lindbergh admired the Bird's flying qualities so much that he bought one to teach his wife how to fly. Eventually Anne Lindbergh soloed the plane at the Aviation Country Club in Hicksville. Of the 220 Birds built, about 60 survive.

The remains of the Model A Bird on display were purchased for the museum by the Friends for Long Island's Heritage at auction in Pennsylvania. The plane was subsequently restored by museum volunteers.

Specifications

Wingspan: 34'
Length: 22' 3"
Engine: 90 HP Curtiss OX-5
Top speed: 105 MPH
Weight: 1,315 lbs

The Bird now on display at the museum, photographed in a Pennsylvania field, ca. 1940.

Curtiss Robin

GARDEN CITY AND ST. LOUIS, MISSOURI, 1929

A Robin equipped with EDO floats, Lake Ronkonkoma, 1932.

In the aviation boom following Lindbergh's flight, one of the most significant airplanes of the 1920s was introduced. It was the Curtiss Robin, a three-place cabin monoplane. Although not a radical advance in design, it did represent a trend that culminated in the modern airplane. As a monoplane it was a distinct departure from previous Curtiss designs, and the enclosed cabin was an innovation.

The Robin was designed as a less expensive alternative to contemporary biplanes of the same weight and power, featuring the comfort of an enclosed cabin and the simplicity of the monoplane. It was designed at the Curtiss factory in Garden City in 1927, the most completely engineered private plane of its day. The Robin's aerodynamics were thoroughly tested in the Curtiss wind tunnel. Profiting from Curtiss's military aircraft experience, the plane was designed with a steel-tube fuselage braced by the Warren truss method, eliminating all wires (and the need to adjust them). The Robin's two passenger seats were side by side, behind the pilot.

The first Robins were built in Garden City, but the bulk of production took place at a new plant in St. Louis. The aircraft was initially powered by World War I surplus Curtiss OX-5 engines, but by 1929 demands for more power were met with the air-cooled Curtiss Challenger engine. Several historic flights were made in Robins, including a world endurance record of over 647 hours (with refueling) in 1930. Most notably, in 1938 Douglas Corrigan departed Floyd Bennett Field, Brooklyn, in a Robin, purportedly heading for California. However, the next day he turned up in Ireland, claiming he had flown the "wrong way." Altogether, 769 Robins were built, more than any other Curtiss model between the wars, making them the most numerous civil aircraft of their day.

The Robin on display was found, in poor condition, in a barn in Maine in 1999. It is exhibited on EDO model 2880 floats which date from the early 1930s. EDO is Long Island's oldest aviation company, having been established in 1925, and was the world's largest manufacturer of aircraft floats from the 1920s to the 1960s.

Specifications

Wingspan: 41'
Length: 25'1"
Engine: 185 HP Curtiss Challenger
Top speed: 120 MPH
Weight: 1,700 lbs.

American Aeronautical (Savoia-Marchetti) S-56

PORT WASHINGTON, 1929

An S-56 about to touch down in Manhasset Bay, ca. 1930.

All aspects of American aviation began to boom after the epic Lindbergh flight of 1927, and many new firms with hastily developed designs emerged to fill the demand for new aircraft. The American Aeronautical Corporation of Port Washington decided to market established foreign designs rather than take the time to develop and certify new ones. The principal design chosen was the Italian Savoia-Marchetti S-56, a three-place amphibian.

The S-56 was a conventional design for the period and one of only two foreign-designed aircraft ever built on Long Island. The hull was a wooden frame covered by plywood, the wings were wood-framed, and the tail was made of steel tube; all were fabric-covered. Basically, the S-56 was a version of the Italian military flying boats used during World War I, now equipped with hand-cranked retractable landing gear and a new 100-HP Kinner K-5 engine in place of the Italian version of the French Anzani originally used.

Most private flying was still open-cockpit in those days, and the S-56 carried its three occupants in a single cockpit centered under the upper wing. The pilot and one passenger sat side by side in front, with the third seat behind them. However, as the plane was underpowered, a third person was rarely carried. While most of the biplane flying boat types of the period were pushers, the S-56 was a notable exception in being a tractor. Its original price was $7,000.

Like many designs of the period, the S-56 succumbed to the Depression, with only about thirty being built. In order to construct the amphibians in Port Washington, the American Aeronautical Corporation put up a new hangar/ factory on Manhasset Bay in 1929. This same facility was later used by Pan American for their transatlantic flying boat operations. The S-56s achieved some measure of fame as the first aircraft to be used by the New York City Police Department, in 1929, which used them to enforce flying regulations and for rescues at sea.

The S-56 on display was based at Roosevelt Field for the first years of its flying career; it later operated on Lake Erie. One of two remaining S-56s, it was located in poor condition in a barn in New Jersey. Museum volunteers restored it over an eight-year period.

On loan from Mr. Ralph Cox.

Specifications

Wingspan: 34'2"
Length: 25'7"
Engine: 100 HP Kinner K-5
Top speed: 92 MPH
Weight: 1,100 lbs

An S-56 in front of its Port Washington factory.

Consolidated Fleet Model 2

BUFFALO, NEW YORK, 1929

The Fleet Model 2 now on display at the museum, photographed at Roosevelt Field, ca. 1930.

Designed by Reuben Fleet and built by Consolidated Aircraft, the Fleet 2 was originally a training plane for the U.S. Army and Navy. Equipped with a 90-HP Kinner engine, the Fleet featured a welded steel tubing fuselage and wings with aluminum ribs, all covered in fabric. With a cruising speed of 90 MPH, the Fleet was a strong, stable, maneuverable training plane that was extremely popular in the late 1920s and early 1930s. A total of 270 were built.

The Roosevelt Aviation School was established in the late 1920s at Roosevelt Field (where the mall now stands). The school quickly became one of the largest and most famous training centers for pilots and mechanics in the United States. Roosevelt Field itself was known as the world's premier airport during the 1930s, the Golden Age of aviation. The school's first training aircraft were five Fleet Model 2s. A small, two-seat, open-cockpit biplane, the Fleet was viewed with affection by students and instructors alike. Among the many pilots trained at the Roosevelt Aviation School was Jacqueline Cochran, who later set many speed records during the 1930s and won several notable air races.

The aircraft on display, numbered NC614M, was the school's night-flying trainer—as evidenced by the teardrop-shaped landing lights, unusual for an airplane of this period. Among the many pilots who soloed on this aircraft was museum founder George Dade, who performed his first loop in it in 1929. The old aircraft was sold off, along with its runway mates, to private individuals in 1945. Fortunately, after many years of abandonment, it was found in upstate New York by museum staff, and purchased for the museum by the Friends for Long Island's Heritage. Obtained in very poor condition, it was restored over a four-year period by museum volunteers. The Fleet is now configured as it was when operated by the Roosevelt Field School in 1930.

Specifications

Wingspan: 28'
Length: 20'9"
Engine: 90 HP Kinner K-5
Top speed: 110 MPH
Weight: 1,035 lbs

Peel Z-1 Glider Boat

COLLEGE POINT, QUEENS, 1930

After the epochal 1927 flight of Charles Lindbergh from Long Island to Paris, a wave of flying fever swept the country. As the price of conventional aircraft was still far above what the average person could afford, this inspired a number of manufacturers to develop simple, low-cost gliders. One of these manufacturers was the Peel Glider Boat Corporation of College Point, Queens. Peel built a prototype biplane glider flying boat at Roosevelt Field, with full production shifted to College Point in 1929. The aircraft was first demonstrated in Manhasset Bay by famed aviator Captain Frank Hawks. Priced at $595, this was the only American glider with a boatlike hull.

Peels were intended to be towed aloft behind a speedboat. At around 1,000 feet of altitude, the towrope would be released and the glider would soar off on its own, eventually landing on the water. With an 18-to-1 glide ratio, the Peel could glide nearly 3.5 miles after being released from a thousand-foot towline. The dual-control glider featured a riveted-aluminum hull and wooden wings covered in fabric. Only thirty Peel Glider Boats were built before the company went out of business in the Depression. The most famous use of a Peel Glider Boat occurred in July 1930, when two Queens pilots attempted to span the Atlantic in their Peel, towed behind the Italian ocean liner *Saturnia*. This would have been the first crossing of the Atlantic by glider, but it ended in failure when the towrope broke only eight hours out of New York.

The Peel was a well-balanced aircraft and quite easy to fly, but it had two distinct drawbacks: first, if it sat in the water too long, water would leak into the hull and shift back to the tail on takeoff, making the aircraft unmanageable; second, the towrope could be released only when it was taut, which could spell disaster if the towboat stalled.

The aircraft on display is the sole surviving example of the Peel Glider Boat. After being found in poor condition in upstate New York, it was thoroughly restored by museum volunteers.

Specifications

Wingspan: 31'
Length: 22'
Top speed: 30 MPH
Weight: 270 lbs

A Z-1 Glider Boat being launched in Manhasset Bay, ca. 1935.

Grumman F3F-2

BETHPAGE, 1938 (replica)

In 1935 the U.S. Navy placed an order with the Grumman Aircraft Engineering Corporation, then of Farmingdale, for the design and construction of a new fighter, the F3F. Based on earlier Grumman biplane designs, the F3F was faster and more maneuverable than any Navy fighter to date. By 1937, due to the slow development of the early monoplane fighters, the Navy ordered more F3Fs, this time an improved model, the F3F-2. The F3F-2 was strong, fast, maneuverable, and was considered a wonderful aircraft to fly. Its pilots considered it the ultimate biplane fighter; in fact it was the last biplane fighter produced in the United States. With its silver fuselage, yellow wings, and red, white, and blue markings, it was among the most colorful military aircraft ever built, but it heralded the end of an era.

By 1939 all U.S. Navy and Marine fighter squadrons flew Grumman biplane fighters exclusively. Of the 164 F3Fs built, 140 were still in service, as trainers in the United States, at the time of the U.S. entry into World War II in December, 1941. Today the F3F is an extremely rare aircraft, with but two original surviving examples.

The aircraft is an accurate full-scale interactive replica of the F3F, built by museum volunteers working from original blueprints.

Specifications

Wingspan: 32'
Length: 23'3"
Engine: Wright R-1820, 950 HP
Top speed: 264 MPH
Weight: 4,116 lbs

An F3F-2 in U.S. Marine Corps markings, ca. 1938.

Grumman G-21 Goose

BETHPAGE, 1938

The Goose taking off, ca. 1940s.

In 1936, the Grumman Aircraft Corporation of Bethpage was approached by several wealthy Long Island residents who needed a small plane for personal transportation. They wanted an aircraft large enough to carry their families and baggage on trips, luxurious enough to fit their business needs, and flexible enough to take off and land either from the land or the sea. These men intended to leave from the water that bordered their Long Island mansions and fly as commuters to a seaplane base at the foot of Wall Street.

Grumman responded with the Goose. First flown in 1937, this twin-engine amphibian offered dependable, economical transport and could be operated from small fields, lakes, and harbors. The aircraft represents a 1930s transitional design, with most of the structure made of riveted aluminum and the aft sections of the wings and control surfaces covered in fabric. The Goose carried six to eight persons and was intended for use by corporate and private owners and charter operators. Despite the aircraft's $60,000 purchase price, it was an immediate success. It was a true forerunner of today's executive jets. Owners could custom-tailor the Goose to fit their needs and pocketbooks. A galley and a lavatory were typically included. Although the Goose was Grumman's first civil design, the armed forces became the major customer, with the Navy buying 205 during World War II for transport and search

and rescue work. A total of 345 were built from 1937 to 1945. The Goose was a very successful and enduring airplane and a surprisingly large number are still flying all over the world.

The Goose on display had a long career in the air, including extensive use as "Cutter's Goose" on the television series *Tales of the Gold Monkey* in the mid-1970s. It is unknown who this aircraft was originally built for, but a repair tag indicates that at one time, probably in the 1950s, it was operated by Antilles Air Boats in the Caribbean. A museum staff member eventually found it moldering on the back lot of Universal Studios in Hollywood. It was purchased for the museum by the Friends for Long Island's Heritage. It was subsequently restored by museum volunteers and is now configured as one of the Pan American "Baby Clippers" that were used for short routes in the Caribbean in the 1940s.

Specifications

Wingspan: 49'
Length: 38'6"
Engines: Two 450 HP Pratt & Whitney R-985s
Top speed: 201 MPH
Weight: 5,425 lbs

Grumman F4F-3 Wildcat

BETHPAGE, 1943

When World War II broke out in the Pacific, the Grumman F4F Wildcat was the main fighter aircraft available to the U.S. Navy and Marine Corps. Wildcats held the line in the Pacific for the first two years of the war, although often outnumbered and pitted against aircraft of superior performance. The F4F's major opponent was the Japanese Zero, a fighter that could outmaneuver and outperform it, but the Wildcat's heavy armament and solid construction gave it an advantage in the hands of skilled pilots.

The F4F Wildcat, first flown in 1937, was developed from an earlier Grumman Navy biplane fighter, the F3F. The F4F-3 was a fixed-wing design, while the F4F-4 featured folding wings, so that more could be fit on board aircraft carriers. Production models were provided not only to the U.S. Navy and Marine Corps, but also to the British Royal Navy, where the F4F was called the Martlet.

Throughout the Pacific the tough little Wildcat had a kill average for the war of nearly seven to one. In February 1942 Lt. Cmdr. "Butch" O'Hare, flying an F4F, shot down five Japanese bombers attacking the U.S. aircraft carrier *Lexington*, to win the Congressional Medal of Honor.

When a new Grumman fighter, the F6F Hellcat, was developed to replace the Wildcat as the Navy's primary fighter, the Navy still needed Wildcats for the smaller escort carriers. To make room for Hellcat production at the Grumman plant, F4F manufacture was turned over to the Eastern Aircraft Division of General Motors, which designated them the FM-1 and FM-2. A total of nearly 8,000 Wildcats were built.

Not many Wildcats have survived. The F4F-3 on display crashed into Lake Michigan during carrier training exercises in January 1944. During World War II the U.S. Navy converted two paddle-wheel steamships into 500-foot-long aircraft carriers. These small carriers were used to qualify 17,800 pilots for carrier landings. On January 16, 1944, Ensign Horace Little was coming in for his first-ever carrier landing when, about two feet above the deck, he elected to go around again. Unfortunately, he did not realize that his tailhook had already caught an arresting wire. As the aircraft surged forward at full power, the tail broke off due to the strain, after which the rest of the plane sailed over the ship's side. Ensign Little was immediately recovered with no injuries. His aircraft was not recovered until 1989 when a salvage operation raised it. The recovery effort was funded by the Friends for Long Island's Heritage. The Wildcat was restored to its original appearance by the Grumman Retiree Group and museum volunteers over an eight-year period.

On loan from the National Museum of Naval Aviation.

Specifications

Wingspan: 38'
Length: 28'9"
Engine: 1,200 HP Pratt & Whitney R-1830-86
Top speed: 320 MPH
Weight: 5,758 lbs

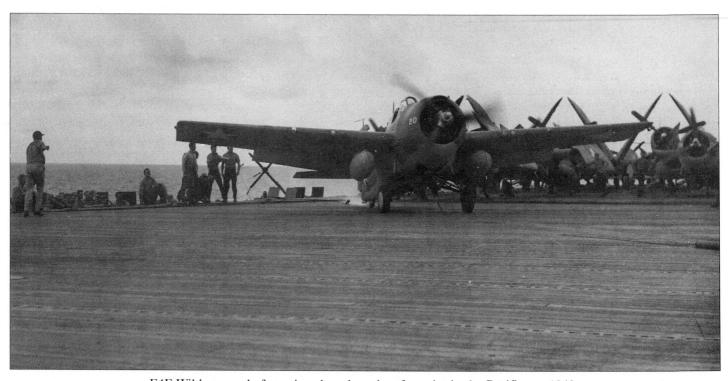

F4F Wildcats ready for action aboard an aircraft carrier in the Pacific, ca. 1943.

An F4F Wildcat in flight, 1943.

Grumman F6F-5 Hellcat

BETHPAGE, 1945

The U.S. Navy's best carrier-based fighter in World War II was without a doubt the Grumman F6F Hellcat. A larger and more powerful development of the earlier Grumman F4F Wildcat, the Hellcat was designed around the new high-powered R-2800 engine. Grumman's engineering team, led by William Schwendler, designed the F6F to counter Japan's excellent Zero fighter. The Hellcat was armed with six .50-caliber machine guns as well as rockets, and the wings folded flat against the fuselage to make the most of the limited space on board aircraft carriers. The Hellcat's design sacrificed speed for a high rate of climb and exceptional maneuverability. It was also a very rugged and well-armored design.

The Hellcat first flew in June 1942 and was deployed in the Pacific in August 1943. For the next two years it participated in every major engagement of the war. The F6F-5 version entered production in 1944 and operated as a fighter-bomber, with underwing rockets and bombs. At one point in 1944 Grumman was turning out one Hellcat per hour—644 per month—with a workforce mostly of women. This aircraft production record has never been equaled. The Hellcat was also the only American fighter ever developed that required no further modifications before it could successfully engage in combat.

Hellcats had a remarkable 19-1 "kill ratio," with 19 enemy planes destroyed for every Hellcat downed. They are given credit for 75 percent of all Japanese aircraft destroyed in the Pacific—no fewer than 5,156. The grand total of Hellcats built through November 1945 was 12,275, all at Grumman's Bethpage plant.

The Hellcat on display was delivered to the Navy in July 1945, just a month before Japan surrendered. It was based at San Diego, Pensacola, Norfolk, and New York (at Floyd Bennett Field) until 1948, when it was placed in storage in North Carolina. It has been repainted in the markings of Marine Squadron VMF-511, which operated from the escort carrier USS *Block Island* in 1945.

On loan from the U.S. Marine Corps Museum.

Specifications

Wingspan: 42'10"
Length: 33'7"
Engine: 2,000 HP Pratt & Whitney R-2800
Top speed: 375 MPH
Weight: 9,101 lbs

Row after row of F6F Hellcats aboard an aircraft carrier in the Pacfiic, 1945.

Crew members aboard an aircraft carrier hustle to tend an F6F Hellcat.

Grumman TBM-3E Avenger

BETHPAGE AND TRENTON, NEW JERSEY, 1945

The famed TBF was contracted for by the U.S. Navy in 1940 as a replacement torpedo bomber for the aging TBD-1 Devastator. Grumman based its design on a scaled-up F4F Wildcat, adding foldable wings to save space on aircraft carriers. A production contract for 286 Avengers was placed in December 1940, although the first flight of the XTBF-1 was not until August 1941. The first public showing of the TBF was on December 7, 1941, at a Grumman "open house." In light of the events in Pearl Harbor that day the aircraft was subsequently named the "Avenger." Grumman delivered 145 production TBF-1s in the first half of 1942, six going to squadron VT-8 and flying from Midway Island on June 4, 1942, in the famous Battle of Midway.

Flying from aircraft carriers and land bases, Avengers became the standard torpedo bombers of World War II. Most operated in the Pacific but some saw action in the Atlantic with American and Allied forces. The Avenger carried a crew of three and could carry a torpedo, bombs, mines or depth charges in its bomb bay. The aircraft also featured a Grumman-designed power turret. The great naval battles of World War II became, in the main, contests between opposing fleets of aircraft. As the American forces grew in numbers and efficiency, carrier-type attack planes accounted for six of the ten Japanese battleships sunk during the war, as well as eleven of fifteen carriers and ten of fourteen heavy cruisers destroyed. Aircraft such as the Avenger destroyed the Japanese Navy, virtually ended the era of the battleship, and established a naval superiority over the rest of the world such as had never before been seen.

Grumman's production of Avengers, largely by women war workers, continued at Bethpage until 1944, totaling 2,293 planes. In 1942 General Motors was contracted to manufacture the aircraft as the TBM, freeing Grumman to produce F6F Hellcats. GM produced 2,882 TBM-1s and 4,664 as TBM-3s, bringing total Avenger production to 9,839.

The Avenger on display was accepted by the U.S. Navy in August 1945 and served with several squadrons, including VMTB-624. It logged over 1,500 military flight hours before being retired from the Navy in 1954. It

A team of women works on the fuselage of an Avenger, Bethpage, 1942.

was then modified to serve as a crop-duster and firefighting water bomber in the Pacific Northwest until 1981. The aircraft was purchased for the museum by the Friends for Long Island's Heritage, sponsored by Mrs. William Schwendler. Flown from Idaho to Bethpage in 1987 with barely functional power and hydraulic systems, it was then restored to its World War II appearance by the Grumman Retiree Group.

Specifications

Wingspan: 54'2"
Length: 40'
Engine: 1,700 HP Wright R-2600
Top Speed: 271 MPH
Weight: 10,080 lbs

TBF Avengers fly over an *Essex*-class aircraft carrier, 1943.

Republic P-47N Thunderbolt

FARMINGDALE, 1945

Without question, the P-47 was one of America's greatest fighters of World War II. The aircraft was designed by Republic Aviation's engineering genius Alexander Kartveli, who built the plane around the powerful new R-2800 engine. The Thunderbolt had the advantage of being equipped with a turbo-supercharger, greatly enhancing its high-altitude performance. Built by Republic in Farmingdale, it made its first flight on May 6, 1941, although the Air Corps placed orders for almost 800 before the prototype even made its first flight. On April 8, 1943, the Thunderbolt flew its first combat mission in Europe, and over the next several months, Air Corps pilots learned that the Thunderbolt could easily outdive any Luftwaffe plane. An external fuel tank was added in July 1943, permitting the P-47 to escort heavy bombers much farther into German territory.

Armed with eight .50-caliber machine guns, the P-47 carried more firepower than any other fighter in World War II. Although it was the largest and heaviest American single-seat fighter to see combat, its huge Pratt & Whitney 18-cylinder engine easily compensated for its size and weight. The leading American air combat unit in Europe, the 56th Fighter Group, compiled a remarkable record with its P-47s: 1,006 German planes destroyed at a cost of only 128 of their own. The two leading American aces in Europe, Bob Johnson and Francis Gabreski, both flew P-47s exclusively.

In addition to establishing an impressive record as a high-altitude escort fighter, the P-47 gained recognition as a low-level fighter-bomber because of its ability to carry a heavy ordnance load (up to two tons of rockets and bombs) and to absorb battle damage and keep flying. The Thunderbolt was widely used in both the European and Pacific theaters of war. Over 15,500 P-47s—more than any other U.S. fighter in history—were built by a workforce that was predominately female. At one point in 1944 Republic was turning out 28 P-47s per day.

The P-47 on display—the last one ever built—is an N model, designed for long-range use in the Pacific. The aircraft served first with the Air Force, then with the Pennsylvania Air National Guard, before being retired in 1954. It has been repainted with the markings of Lt. Durwood Williams of the 318th Fighter Group, based on Ie Shima, just west of Okinawa, in the spring of 1945.

On loan from the U.S. Air Force Museum.

Specifications

Wingspan: 40'9"
Length: 36'1"
Top speed: 430 MPH
Engine: 2,300 HP Pratt & Whitney R-2800-21
Weight: 10,700 lbs

A P47 Thunderbolt on a test flight over Long Island, 1944.

Equipped with wing-mounted rockets and machine guns, a P47 Thunderbolt gets ready for takeoff.

Waco CG-4A Glider

MINEOLA AND QUEENS, 1945

The CG-4A was the most widely used U.S. troop and cargo glider of World War II. Flight testing began in 1942, and during the next few years more than 14,000 CG-4As were produced. Seventeen companies manufactured them. On Long Island they were built by Dade Brothers in Mineola (wings) and General Aircraft in Queens (fuselage and tail).

The CG-4A was constructed of steel-tubing fuselage and a wooden wing, both fabric-covered. Crewed by a pilot and copilot, it could carry thirteen soldiers and their equipment—or either a jeep or a 75mm howitzer cannon, loaded through the upward-hinged nose section. C-46s and C-47s were usually used as tow aircraft. A typical function of the glider was to transport its heavily armed troops behind enemy lines, where they could disrupt the advance of the enemy's reserve troops by destroying railroads, bridges, and other communications links. When the gliders came close to their destinations, they were released to complete their one-way mission on their own. A large percentage of glider flights ended in crash landings. In fact, if the landing area proved too small, pilots were instructed to land between two large trees, shearing off the wings and bringing the craft to an abrupt halt.

CG-4As went into operation in July 1943 during the Allied invasion of Sicily. They later participated in the D-Day assault on on June 6, 1944, in other important airborne operations in Europe and in the China-Burma-India Theater. Until late in the war gliders were considered expendable in combat and were abandoned or destroyed after landing. Glider landings were very hazardous due to antiaircraft fire, air traffic congestion in very limited spaces and all kinds of obstructions, and flying them was not considered desirable duty.

The CG-4 on display was dug out of the woods in eastern Pennsylvania in 1989. It had been discarded as worthless in 1946. In poor condition, the aircraft was restored by museum volunteers over a six-year period. It is one of only four surviving CG-4s.

Specifications

Wingspan: 83'8"
Length: 48'4"
Top speed: 150 MPH (towed)
Weight: 4,200 lbs

A CG-4 glider, 1944.

Grumman G-63 Kitten

BETHPAGE, 1944

One of two Grumman Kittens, Bethpage, 1946.

The first Grumman venture in designing a light plane for the private flier can best be described as a successful failure. The project was begun in 1943 as part of Leroy Grumman's search for possible non-military products for the postwar period. Grumman believed that the recent advances in aeronautical technology, including design and manufacturing techniques and power plant development, had made it possible to produce a new type of high-performance light plane. As for the market, it was reasoned that thousands of veteran flyers would be coming home with money in their pockets and a desire to do some personal flying. This reasoning was shared by a number of companies already in the business of building light planes. Grumman's project was staffed by a group of engineers and manufacturing experts headed by Hank Kurt and Dayton T. Brown (designer of the Brewster Buffalo). There was no question that Grumman could produce a good airplane, but there was considerable doubt about the development of a proper market.

The Grumman staff designed a small, two-seat, all-metal, low-wing monoplane equipped with a retractable landing gear and powered by a 125-hp engine. The pretty little aircraft, spot-welded aluminum throughout, bears a family resemblance to the Grumman Wildcat. In the tradition of naming Grumman aircraft after members of the cat family, it

was called the Kitten. Flown for the first time in March 1944 it was in many respects superior to other light planes of the period. Grumman, however, decided not to place the Kitten into production. The expansion of the postwar private airplane market never reached the level that had been anticipated. In fact, many companies that gambled on producing new civilian aircraft soon went out of business. Veterans were more interested in buying houses than in getting airborne. In the end, only two Kittens were made.

The aircraft on display is the only Kitten still in existence. It was used by Grumman as an executive transport into the early 1960s, at which time it was dismantled and placed in storage. It was restored for the museum by the Grumman Retirees Program in the late 1980s.

Donated by Grumman Aerospace Corporation.

Specifications

Wingspan: 32'
Length: 21'
Engine: 125 HP O-290 Lycoming
Top speed: 159 MPH
Weight: 1,200 lbs

Republic RC-3 Seabee

FARMINGDALE, 1947

With the end of World War II in sight, Republic saw the need to produce something other than military aircraft. Thus, company designers initiated the Seabee, a civilian amphibian, for what was foreseen as a booming market for private aircraft in the postwar years. Designed to be built quickly and cheaply, the Seabee was one of the most promising designs to emerge from the huge number of personal aircraft on industry drawing boards. Developed from the Amityville-built Spencer Amphibian Air Car of 1940, Republic's new airplane seemed destined for success, particularly since there was no other low-priced amphibian on the market. Republic's managers believed that there were good prospects for low-cost, mass-produced aircraft in the postwar market, just as there were for the automobile after World War I.

Republic worked to keep the price of the plane low by using as many automobile parts as possible, along with a ribless wing with stiffened skin for strength and a hull with few internal connecting members (a technique known as monocoque construction). The entire airframe was made up of only 450 parts. The four-seat cabin was large and comfortable, with interior fittings resembling the latest in automobile design. The Seabee was powered by a 215-HP Franklin air-cooled pusher engine, located above and to the rear of the cabin not only for greater safety in landing and docking but also to protect it from water spray, to reduce noise, and to provide better forward visibility.

Despite all the expectations and publicity, the postwar aircraft boom failed to materialize, and all who entered the market lost money. A national recession, combined with the availability of cheap military surplus aircraft, killed the Seabee. Volume production was scheduled to start in April 1946, with a goal of 5,000 aircraft in the first year. The unrealistic original price of $3,995 soon escalated to $6,000, putting the aircraft beyond the reach of its intended customers. In early 1948 the final Seabee came off the assembly line; only 1,076 had been produced.

In spite of being underpowered, the Seabee was a solid, safe aircraft that represented a gallant effort to put an extremely flexible aircraft on the market at the lowest possible price. As a testament to its design and construction, over one-third of the original Seabees built are still flying today.

Donated by Mr. Leo Hausman.

Specifications

Wingspan: 37'8"
Length: 28'
Engine: 215 HP Franklin 6A8
Top speed: 120 MPH
Weight: 1,950 lbs.

A Seabee flying smoothly above a scenic inlet—a postwar dream of private flight that was rarely realized.

Getting ready to disembark from a Seabee.

Commonwealth 185 Skyranger

VALLEY STREAM, 1946

At the end of World War II, with no new military aircraft orders in sight, Commonwealth Aircraft of Kansas City bought out the Columbia Aircraft Corporation, which had its plant at Curtiss Field in Valley Stream. Commonwealth anticipated a postwar boom in civil aviation and wanted to use the Valley Stream facility to construct small, low-cost, two-seat private airplanes. But the boom never came, and Commonwealth halted production after a year in 1946, and declared bankruptcy in 1947. Similarly, Grumman's Kitten and Republic's Seabee both failed in the depressed postwar civil aviation market.

In all, Commonwealth constructed 275 Skyrangers, a Piper Cub-sized aircraft, in Valley Stream. About 100 are still flying today. The Skyranger prototype was designed for Rearwin in 1939 and first flew in 1940. Designed for the sportsman pilot, the Skyranger Model 185 seated two, side by side, and featured a steel-tube fuselage and wooden wing, both fabric-covered. The aircraft's unusually large vertical fin and rudder gave it excellent directional stability but made it difficult to land in a crosswind. The price was about $3,000.

The aircraft on display was donated to the museum by Ray Newman of East Haddam, Connecticut in 1986. It was flown to Republic Airport, Farmingdale, and trucked to the museum. It is unaltered from when it last flew.

Specifications

Wingspan: 34'
Length: 21'9"
Engine: 85 HP Continental
Top speed: 110 MPH
Weight: 1,022 lbs.

A publicity photo of a Skyranger, ca. 1946.

Republic P-84B Thunderjet

FARMINGDALE, 1947

A Thunderjet in flight, 1946.

The first new American fighter to fly following the end of World War II was the jet-powered Republic P-84. The origins of this plane go back to 1944, during the frenzied American effort to get a jet fighter into production as German jets began to appear in the skies over Europe. At first, because jet airframe and engine development were lagging, the Air Corps asked Republic to redesign the P-47 around an axial-flow turbojet engine. After the preliminary designs were completed, Republic deemed the entire idea impractical and recommended that an all-new jet aircraft be created. The P-84 was thus designed from scratch around what was then an advanced turbojet engine, the GE-TG-180, later redesignated the Allison J-35. This was a more streamlined power plant than earlier models. The plane was designed with a direct airflow from a nose intake to the engine via ducting around the cockpit, and out the tail.

On November 11, 1944, the Air Corps accepted Republic's plans, and the XP-84 made its first flight at Muroc Field (now Edwards AFB), California, on February 28, 1946. A second XP-84 was flown on September 6, 1946, to a new world-record speed of 611 mph, even more impressive in that it was achieved by a standard production aircraft, not an experimental model. The Air Corps was so pleased with the XP-84 that 85 production P-84Bs were ordered, each to be equipped with six .50-caliber machine guns as well as rockets and bombs. The first production P-84Bs began to reach Air Force units in early 1947. Later models of the Thunderjet, specifically the D and G versions, were vastly superior to the B models. They had more powerful engines and were equipped

with wingtip fuel tanks and rocket-assisted takeoff units. By the time of the Korean War in 1950, Republic was the largest producer of jet fighters in the western world. The Thunderjet model of which the most units (3,025) were produced was the F-84G. This aircraft saw widespread and successful use during the Korean War as a fighter-bomber.

The P-84B on display is the eighth one made and the oldest surviving Long Island-built production jet. It was delivered to the U.S. Air Force in 1947 and served with the 20th Fighter Group in South Carolina, the 181st Fighter Squadron in Texas, and the 116th Fighter Squadron in Washington. Excessed by the Air Force in 1955, it became a ground target at the Naval Weapons Test Center, China Lake (Death Valley), California. It was there that its remains were found, extensively damaged by machine gun fire, rockets and bombs, and rescued by the museum. Funds for the difficult salvage operation were provided by the Friends for Long Island's Heritage. Museum volunteers worked for over four years to restore the aircraft.

On loan from the U.S. Navy.

Specifications

Wingspan: 34'
Length: 38'6"
Top speed: 600 MPH
Engine: 4,000 lb-thrust Allison J-35 turbojet
Weight: 10,090 lbs

43

Republic F-84F Thunderstreak

FARMINGDALE, 1954

As successful as the earlier straight-wing Republic Thunderjets were, they reached their design limits with the F-84G of 1952. Thus Republic proposed, and then developed, a highly refined swept-wing version originally designated the YF-96A. However, because Congress would not fund the development of an all-new fighter, the Air Force simply called the plane an F-84F. Thus, Republic was able to proceed with production of the aircraft even though it bore little resemblance to earlier F-84 versions.

The F-84F was developed as a powerful all-weather fighter-bomber capable of speeds up to 695 MPH. It carried six machine guns and a supply of bombs and rockets; it was also capable of delivering nuclear weapons. A total of 2,711 Thunderstreaks were built between 1952 and 1957. Not only did the U.S. Air Force deploy this aircraft, it was also one of the most widely exported Long Island-built fighter, used by the air forces of France, Belgium, Holland, Italy, West Germany, Greece and Turkey. The only F-84Fs to see combat were those flown by the French Air Force, which went into action against Egypt during the Suez Crisis of 1956.

In March 1955 an F-84F piloted by Lt. Col. Robert Scott set a transcontinental speed record, flying from Los Angeles to Mitchel Field in 3 hours, 44 minutes. A reconnaissance version of the Thunderstreak, the RF-84F, featured engine air intakes at the wing roots plus cameras in the nose.

The F-84F on display belonged to the U.S. Air Force until 1959, when it was turned over to the 104th Tactical Fighter Group of the Massachusetts Air National Guard. In the mid-1960s the aircraft was on a cross-country training flight when engine trouble forced it to land at Portland, Oregon. Rather than make the old aircraft flyable, the Air Force elected to abandon it in place. It was disassembled by volunteers and transported across country to the museum in 1985.

On loan from the U.S. Air Force Museum.

Specifications

Wingspan: 33'7"
Length: 43'4"
Engine: 7,200 lb-thrust Wright J-65
Top Speed: 695 MPH
Weight: 17,000 lbs

A Thunderstreak taking off from Republic Airport.

Republic F-105B Thunderchief

FARMINGDALE, 1958

An F-105D Thunderchief, named *The Jolly Roger*, ready for takeoff from an airstrip in Vietnam.

The F-105 evolved from a project begun in 1951 by Republic Aviation to develop an advanced long-range supersonic aircraft specifically for the delivery of nuclear weapons. The prototype first flew in 1955, and a first run of 75 F-105Bs was built. Total F-105 production, ending in 1964, reached 833 aircraft, mostly D model all-weather fighter-bombers and two-seat F model electronic warfare aircraft. The F-105 was notable for its large bomb bay and unique swept-forward engine inlets in the wing roots. The Thunderchief is still the largest single-engine, single-seat aircraft ever built. Top speed was a remarkable 1,264 MPH.

The F-105 fighter-bomber proved its worth when it was pushed into service in Vietnam, even though it was used as a tactical strike aircraft, a role for which it was not designed. Despite adverse climate and combat conditions, the F-105 demonstrated its durability. It was generally equipped with a 20mm Vulcan cannon in the nose (able to fire 6,000 rounds per minute) and up to 16,750 pounds of bombs or rockets (Sidewinders, Bullpups, or Shrikes) on external mounts. The "Thud," as it was nicknamed, quickly became the workhorse of the USAF, used for 75 percent of its strike missions in Vietnam. The F-105 was also used as a bomber, and the usual load it carried exceeded by 50 percent the amount carried by a B-17 in World War II. The attitude of the Thunderchief's crews quickly changed from dislike to admiration as the plane revealed an ability to sus-

tain heavy battle damage and still return home safely. It was particularly effective in the "Wild Weasel" role, as a SAM (surface-to-air missile) site destroyer. In smashing railways, blowing up bridges, destroying steel mills, and even tangling with Migs, the F-105 wrote itself into the pages of aviation history. On flights over North Vietnam, F-105s would face not only Migs, but also surface-to-air missiles, intense antiaircraft flak, and even automatic weapons fire. This was the most intense combat environment ever encountered to that time.

The F-105 on display is an early B model that was never used in combat. It was part of the U.S. Air Force until 1972, when it was turned over to the New Jersey Air National Guard. Upon its retirement in 1980 the aircraft was flown to Republic Airport in Farmingdale, then trucked down Hempstead Turnpike to the museum.

On loan from the U. S. Air Force Museum.

Specifications

Wingspan: 34'11"
Length: 64'3"
Engine: 26,500 lb-thrust Pratt & Whitney J-75-P-19 turbojet
Top Speed: 1,264 MPH; 1,420 MPH with afterburner
Weight: 27,500 lbs

Convertawings Model A Quadrotor

AMITYVILLE, 1956

The Convertawings Company was organized in 1950 by a group of aircraft designers headed by D. H. Kaplan. Their primary interest was in the development of experimental vertical flight aircraft. Located at Zahn's Airport, Amityville, Convertawings set out to develop a unique high-lift, high-speed helicopter that would not have a tail rotor and that would make use of small wings for added lift in forward flight. Their aircraft featured two four-cylinder engines driving four rotors with simplified propeller hubs. Control was obtained by varying the thrust between rotors, thus eliminating the standard helicopter cyclic control. On March 30, 1956, the Quadrotor first flew. During this and subsequent tests the helicopter hovered; flew sideways, backward and forward; and made quick stops from over 50 MPH. Successful performance of this test machine provided conclusive proof not only that the Quadrotor configuration was workable but also that it offered the means for a basic improvement in the helicopter. The Convertawings Model A was also the first four-rotor helicopter to demonstrate successful forward flight. It was created as the prototype for much larger heavy-lift passenger and cargo quadrotors.

Despite successful testing and development, however, military support for the Quadrotor ceased after cutbacks in defense spending during the late 1950s. Convertawings was shut down, and the $1million spent on the project was written off as a loss. D. H. Kaplan moved on to work for Bell Helicopter, where he ultimately became one of the lead designers on the V-22 Osprey, and the helicopter itself was cut up and buried. Nevertheless, the design, particularly of its control system, proved to be an important precursor of current experimental vertical rising aircraft designs, which incorporate tandem wings with fans, ducts, or jets.

The aircraft on display was unearthed at Zahn's Airport and restored by museum volunteers in the 1980s.

Specifications

Rotor Diameter: 19'4"
Length: 26'
Engines: Two 90 HP Continentals
Top speed: 80 MPH
Weight: 2,200 lbs

The Convertawings Model A on its first free flight, March 30, 1956.

Gyrodyne Model 2C

ST. JAMES, 1952

The Model 2C, nicknamed "the eggbeater," during final tests at St. James.

The Gyrodyne Company of America was founded in 1946 by Peter Papadakos to investigate advanced helicopter designs with the goal of producing a better rotary-wing aircraft than any being offered at that time. After a period of research, the company became intrigued with the potential of a coaxial configuration—a design that uses two counter-rotating sets of blades in order to eliminate rotor torque and thus the need for a tail rotor. A small hangar facility was leased at Fitzmaurice Field, Massapequa. During 1949 Gyrodyne translated theoretical research into practical application by developing the first compound helicopter, or convertiplane. This was the Model 2B, which had side-mounted engines for high-speed forward thrust and a coaxial rotor system for lift. In 1951 Gyrodyne moved to much larger facilities at St. James, where it could both produce and flight-test new helicopters. The company had a contract with the U.S. Navy for a flight-demonstration program to provide comparative data to the Bureau of Aeronautics on the coaxial helicopter. The program soon proved conclusively that the coaxial configuration offered many important advantages. Successful operation of this new type of helicopter, the Model 2C, ultimately led to Gyrodyne's securing several large contracts over the next twenty years for both small manned and unmanned coaxial helicopters.

The aircraft on display is the Model 2C that was used in Gyrodyne's early test flights on Long Island. First flown in April 1952, this aircraft could seat up to six, making it the largest helicopter ever built on Long Island. It was flown continuously through the 1950s, and was then placed in storage at Gyrodyne. In 1993 it was turned over to the museum and restored to its original condition by museum volunteers.

On permanent loan from Gyrodyne Company of America.

Specifications

Rotor diameter: 48'
Width: 12'
Engine: 450 HP Pratt & Whitney R-985
Top speed: 110 MPH
Weight: 3,800 lbs

Gyrodyne XRON Rotorcycle

ST. JAMES, 1955

A Marine XRON, ca. 1956.

In response to a U.S. Navy request for a cheap, simple, one-man helicopter, numerous "flying motorcycles" with various propulsion systems were built in the 1950s. The Gyrodyne Company of America, located in St. James, produced the XRON Rotorcycle between 1954 and 1956. It had a maximum weight of 688 pounds, consisting of counter-rotating (coaxial) rotors, engine, and tricycle landing gear, with pilot and equipment—all mounted on a tubular fuselage. The XRON had a respectable top speed of 70 MPH. Gyrodyne built fifteen Rotorcycles, which were evaluated by the Marines as reconnaissance and one-man assault helicopters. A later unmanned derivative was produced in large numbers for the U.S. Navy in the 1960s.

One unusual feature of the XRON was the use of small rotor tip-mounted drag brakes as a means of directional control and stabilization. The brakes turned the fuselage by unbalancing the torque of the counter-rotating rotors. The XRON was extremely maneuverable, and was designed to be flown by personnel with minimal training.

The XRON on display is one of only three survivors, a rare example of the aircraft produced by the once highly active helicopter industry on Long Island. The Friends for Long Island's Heritage purchased it as surplus, in flyable condition, from the U.S. Department of Defense.

Specifications

Rotor diameter: 17'
Length: 11'
Engine: 62 HP Porsche YO-95
Top speed: 71 MPH
Weight: 430 lbs

Gyrodyne QH-50C DASH

ST. JAMES, 1967

The Gyrodyne Company embarked on the development of coaxial helicopters from its inception. In 1960 the company designed, built, and demonstrated for the U.S. Navy a small remote-controlled helicopter for use in combating the growing Soviet submarine threat. Successful demonstrations of this machine marked the first-ever free flight of a completely unmanned drone helicopter. The helicopter, called a DASH (Drone Anti-Submarine Helicopter), was a radio-controlled craft launched from a destroyer to attack submarines while the ship itself remained outside the lethal range of the target. The initiative for the drone weapon system grew from Navy's desire to extend the useful life of World War II destroyers. The DASH system provided the destroyers with a flexible, deliberate, long-range attack capability against submarines.

The production model of the DASH was designated the QH-50C. It was first delivered to the U.S. fleet in 1962, powered by a 290-hp Boeing engine and armed with two Mark 44 acoustic homing torpedoes for "beyond the horizon" operation. After a DASH was launched, it was tracked by radar on the "homing" ship and was remotely guided by signals to the enemy submarine, whose location was detected by sonar. The DASH then launched its torpedoes and was flown back to the ship for reuse. Approximately 700 QH-50 type helicopters were built in St. James between 1960 and 1968. At one time they were carried on more than 100 antisubmarine vessels. They were last operational in 1975.

The DASH on display was originally assigned to the destroyer USS *Stickell* (DD-888). It was obtained by the museum from the Army's Aberdeen Proving Ground, Maryland, just before it was to be destroyed. Museum volunteers restored it in 1988.

Specifications

Rotor diameter: 20'
Length: 12'11"
Engine: 290 HP Boeing T-50 turbine
Top speed: 92 MPH
Weight: 1,754 lbs

A QH-50C landing on the destroyer USS *Hazelwood*.

Grumman F9F-7 Cougar

BETHPAGE, 1953

Grumman's Cougar, an advanced design for its time, was evolved from the earlier straight-wing F9F Panther, Grumman's first jet. Panthers were fighter-bombers, the first Navy jets in action in the Korea. During that war they flew nearly half of the Navy's combat missions, mainly in the ground attack role. The Cougar was the Navy's first swept-wing jet which allowed for the highest speeds. It was designed in haste to provide the Navy with a weapon to combat the excellent Mig-15s being encountered in Korea. It first flew in September 1951. The Cougar's easy handling and strong airframe, well suited to the rigors of carrier operations, earned praise from its pilots.

The Cougar was armed with four 20mm cannons and rockets. Under the fuselage it was fitted with dive brakes, which could be extended to slow the plane in flight during bombing runs or for carrier landings. The first transcontinental flight of less than four hours, San Diego to Floyd Bennett Field, was made by three Cougars in April 1954. A total of 1,988 were built, and some remained in service until 1974. Cougars were replaced as front-line jets in the late 1950s, as they were rendered obsolete by rapid technological developments such as supersonic aircraft. However, two-seat versions of the Cougar played a vital role in training most of the naval pilots who flew combat operations in Vietnam. In fact, four Marine two-seat Cougars served as forward air controllers during the Vietnam War in 1966-67, directing strike aircraft against enemy positions. This was the only time Cougars were used in combat.

The Cougar on display was at one time deployed aboard the aircraft carrier USS *Randolph*. It was found as a battered, burned hulk at the Naval Firefighting School, Lakehurst Naval Air Station, New Jersey, and was painstakingly restored by museum volunteers over a three-year period. It is displayed with the markings of a Naval Reserve Squadron stationed at Floyd Bennett Field in the mid-1950s.

On loan from the U.S. Navy.

Specifications

Wingspan: 34'6"
Length: 40'10"
Engine: 7,200 lb-thrust Pratt & Whitney J-48
Top speed: 690 MPH
Weight: 11,000 lbs.

An F9F-6 Cougar seen from above.

Grumman F-11A Tiger

BETHPAGE, 1954

An F-11A in the markings of the U.S. Navy's Blue Angels aerobatic team.

Originally a Cougar variant called the F9F-9, the Tiger was redesignated the F-11F-1 and developed as an entirely new aircraft. It was the first to incorporate the NACA-developed "area rule" concept from design inception. This concept produced the familiar "Coke-bottle"-shaped fuselage, which greatly reduces drag. The Tiger was the first carrier-based fighter with supersonic capability, thanks to the specially shaped fuselage, powerful engine, and very thin wings fitted into the most compact airframe possible. It was armed with four 20mm cannons and four Sidewinder air-to-air missiles.

The traditional Grumman attributes of simplicity and ruggedness were stressed in the design of the Tiger. The top and bottom wing skins were machine milled from single slabs of aluminum, greatly reducing not only the number of parts required, but also time and expense usually involved in complex wing assembly. The wings also served as integral fuel tanks. Another unusual feature of the Tiger was the use of spoilers instead of ailerons for banking and rolling. This permitted flaps to extend the full length of the wing's trailing edge.

The F-11 was first flown in July, 1954, and deliveries of production aircraft began in 1957 (to VA-156, a Navy fighter/attack squadron). Production continued through December 1958; the last of 201 planes built was delivered in 1959.

Five first-line squadrons were equipped with the Tiger, and for a period this was the Navy's fastest shipboard fighter. The Tiger's main drawback was its short range, owing to its high fuel consumption and lack of external fuel tanks. The Navy's Blue Angels aerobatic team flew Tigers for more than ten years. Two Tigers were modified with 15,000 lb-thrust J79 engines, and in 1956 one set a new world speed record of 1,220 MPH (Mach 1.85) and a new world altitude record of more than 76,000 feet.

The aircraft on display was obtained from the Naval Test Center at Patuxent River, Maryland. It was restored by the Grumman Retiree Group and is now displayed with the markings of Captain Norm Gandia, a Long Islander and one-time Blue Angels pilot.

On loan from the U.S. Navy.

Specifications

Wingspan: 31'7"
Length: 44'11"
Engine: 11,000 lb-thrust Wright J-65
Top Speed: 890 MPH
Weight: 13,428 lbs

Grumman OV-1B Mohawk

BETHPAGE, 1962

First built in 1959, the Mohawk was the U.S. Army's only fixed-wing combat aircraft from the mid-1970s through the 1990s. The Mohawk was designed to maintain round-the-clock surveillance over and beyond battlefield front lines. A total of four versions were built; the OV-1A, for visual and photo surveillance; the OV-1B, with added side-looking airborne radar; the OV-1C, with a panoramic camera added to its photo-infrared systems, and the OV-1D with additional cameras and infrared systems. Improved radio navigation aids also enabled all models to operate at night and in all weather conditions.

Thus the OV-1 was a completely integrated battlefield surveillance system, able to supply army field commanders with information on the strength, disposition, and activity of enemy forces. This two-place twin-turboprop aircraft was equipped with photographic and electronic sensors that could monitor enemy operations in daylight, darkness, and bad weather. The OV-1, with its short takeoff and landing capability, could operate from small unimproved fields in forward battle areas and could be maintained without extensive support equipment. Grumman Mohawks remained in Army operation until 1998 and they saw widespread and successful use in both the Vietnam and Persian Gulf Wars. A total of 380 were built.

The aircraft on display was in service in the Army for 20 years and was last used at Grumman as an electronics upgrade test craft.

Donated by Grumman Aerospace Corporation.

Specifications

Wingspan: 48'
Length: 41'
Engines: two Lycoming T53 turboprops, 1,400 HP each
Top speed: 316 MPH
Weight: 11,800 lbs

An OV-1 with surveillance equipment under the fuselage.

Grumman S2F Tracker

BETHPAGE, 1964

An S-2F, photographed in 1969.

Conceived in 1950, when jet aircraft were becoming standard in the U.S. Navy, the propeller-driven Tracker nevertheless went on to have a remarkably long service life. The first Tracker flew in December 1952, the first aircraft that combined the detection equipment and armament to hunt and destroy submarines with the ability operate from an aircraft carrier. Before Trackers went into service in 1954, the Navy had been using single-engine Grumman AF-2 Guardians, working in hunter-killer pairs. One plane detected and located enemy submarines, and the other attacked them. In fact, individual twin-engine Trackers could do it all: they were equipped not only with radar, searchlights, sonobuoys, and Magnetic Anomaly Detectors (MADs) for detection and location, but also with sub-killing weaponry that included depth charges, homing torpedoes, and bombs. The outboard wing panels also folded to the rear to facilitate movement and storage on board aircraft carriers.

Production deliveries began in 1953, and eventually 1,342 Trackers were built for the Navy in sixteen different versions. An enlarged torpedo bay, enhanced passenger and cargo capacity, longer range radar detection capability, and continual upgrading of electronics marked the development of the S-2 series. Deliveries also included 342 Trackers to the armed forces of Canada, Australia, the Netherlands, Brazil, Argentina, Italy, Turkey, Peru, Chile, Norway, Germany, Colombia, Spain, Japan, Korea, Thailand, Uruguay, Venezuela, and Taiwan. S2Fs also saw service during the Vietnam War, where they performed naval gunfire spotting duty. Today Trackers are still being flown by several foreign air forces and as firefighting water bombers in the Pacific Northwest.

The Tracker on display was accepted by the Navy in 1964 and was deployed aboard two aircraft carriers, the USS *Randolph* and the USS *Intrepid*. It was retired in 1975, after being damaged in a fire. It was obtained from the U.S. Navy and restored by museum volunteers.

On loan from the U.S. Navy.

Specifications

Wingspan: 72'7"
Length: 43'6"
Engines: two 1,525 HP Wright R-1820-82s
Top speed: 287 MPH
Weight: 18,315 lbs

Grumman G-164 Agcat

BETHPAGE AND ELMIRA, NEW YORK, 1965

Among the world's major aircraft manufacturers, Grumman was unique for its bold diversification move into the agricultural aircraft market. However, following the successful development of prototypes, Grumman was forced to subcontract the manufacture of production aircraft to Schweizer Aircraft—in-house production would have made the Agcat too expensive. The Agcat was developed in 1956-57 after a market survey found that there would be a demand for a new type of crop-dusting aircraft to replace the obsolete modified biplane trainers then in use. Grumman managers felt that their reputation for building sturdy aircraft would help them, since agricultural aircraft would need to be able to survive the occasional collision with trees and other obstructions.

The design incorporated several features that made the aircraft strong, maneuverable, and easy to maintain. The biplane configuration allowed for a short wingspan, thus keeping wing loading low. Ailerons on all four wing panels gave great manueverability. It was also decided that the aircraft should be adapted for several types of engines, based on their availability. For ease of maintenance, the fuselage was covered with removable panels. Finally, for safety, the cockpit was reinforced so that it would provide protection in case of a turnover.

The first Agcat was flown at Bethpage in 1957, and the type quickly gained acceptance with both large and small operators. To date over 3,000 Agcats have been produced, and the vast majority are still operational. Not only is this the only agricultural aircraft designed and built on Long Island, it is also the most popular ag-plane in the western world.

The museum's Agcat was located in wrecked condition in upstate New York where it had been used for many years as a cropduster.

Specifications

Wingspan: 35'11"
Length: 24'4"
Engine: 220-850 HP radial, various types
Top speed: 147 MPH
Weight; 2,239 lbs

An Agcat crop-dusting from just a few yards off the ground.

Fairchild-Republic T-46 Flight Demonstrator

BOHEMIA, 1981

A full-size U.S. Air Force T-46.

In 1982 the Fairchild-Republic Corporation of Farmingdale won the U.S. Air Force competition to build the next generation trainer for primary flight instruction. Designated the T-46, it was an H-tail, high-wing design with side-by-side seating for two, twin engines, and a pressurized cockpit. Designed with simplicity, stability, and low operating costs in mind, it was expected that the Air Force would purchase 650 of the trainers through 1993 and that the aircraft would serve well into the twenty-first century. Additionally, Republic expected to sell an attack version of the aircraft overseas.

The T-46 first flew in October 1985, and all flight tests were successful. However, due to budget cuts, the Air Force terminated the T-46 program in 1986 after only four aircraft had been built. As it was their only aircraft contract, the Republic Aviation Corporation was forced to close after more than fifty years of continuous production of military aircraft.

The aircraft on display is a fiberglass flight demonstrator designed by Republic and built to a 62 percent scale by Ames Industries in Bohemia. In 1981 it was flown for more than twenty hours over the Mojave Desert in California by Dick Rutan, the well-known test pilot. His mission was to collect information about the flight handling qualities, control surfaces, spin recovery, and other characteristics of the model that would be useful in designing the full-scale T-46. Republic executives also had another purpose: to secure a government contract to build the aircraft.

Donated by Fairchild-Republic Corporation.

Specifications

Wingspan: 21'10"
Length: 18'4"
Top speed: 260 MPH
Engines: two 220 lb-thrust Garrett Microturbo TRS-18
Weight: 842 lbs

Fairchild-Republic A-10 Thunderbolt II

FARMINGDALE, 1977

In 1973 the Fairchild-Republic Corporation of Farmingdale was selected to build the A-10, the first U.S. Air Force plane specifically designed for close air support. Capable of accurately delivering ordnance at low altitude, the A-10 is the most heavily armed, and armored, plane in history. Originally designed to counter Soviet tanks in Europe, the A-10 is equipped with up to 16,000 pounds of Maverick missiles, laser-guided bombs and a seven-barrel 30mm GAU/8A "Gatling gun" cannon able to fire up to 4200 rounds per minute. No attack aircraft in history has ever mounted a gun with the tank-killing capability of the GAU/8A.

The A-10 was also designed to be able to survive in an intense antiaircraft environment including antiaircraft guns and radar-guided and infrared missiles, absorb battle damage, and keep flying. In fact, the A-10 is probably the most difficult plane to shoot down ever built, due to its extreme maneuverability, electronic countermeasures, self-sealing fuel tanks, widely separated jet engines, twin tails, manual backup flight control system and redundant wing spars. The pilot and vital flight control elements are also protected by 1"-thick titanium armor plate. A total of 713 A-10s were built through 1984, at a cost of only $20 million each, and about 300 will serve with the USAF until 2020.

A-10's were widely used in the 1991 Persian Gulf War where they demonstrated their ability as the greatest tank-killing aircraft in history. A total of 144 A-10s were deployed to the Gulf and they flew 8,624 missions with only two losses. They destroyed a total of 967 tanks, 1,026 pieces of artillery, 1,306 trucks, 281 military structures, 53 Scud missiles, 10 aircraft on the ground and two aircraft in the air. Pilots often flew up to three missions per day. In all, A-10s accounted for the destruction of one fourth of Iraq's entire arsenal. Several aircraft survived direct hits from heat-seeking missiles and managed to return to base. A-10s were also extensively used in the Kosovo intervention of 1999.

The A-10 on display is an early production aircraft built in 1977. It served with the 354th Tactical Fighter Wing at Myrtle Beach, South Carolina until 1982, and then with the 45th Tactical Fighter Squadron at Grissom Air Force Base, Indiana until 1992. It spent its last two years as a battle damage repair training aircraft. It is now shown with the markings of Captain Michael Baltzer of Long Island, who flew 33 A-10 missions during the Gulf War.

On loan from the U.S. Air Force Museum.

Specifications

Wingspan: 57'6"
Length: 53'4"
Top speed: 420 MPH
Engines: two General Electric 9,000 lb-thrust TF-34s
Weight: 22,141 lbs

Two A-10s, each equipped with a large ordnance load.

Veligdan Sailplane

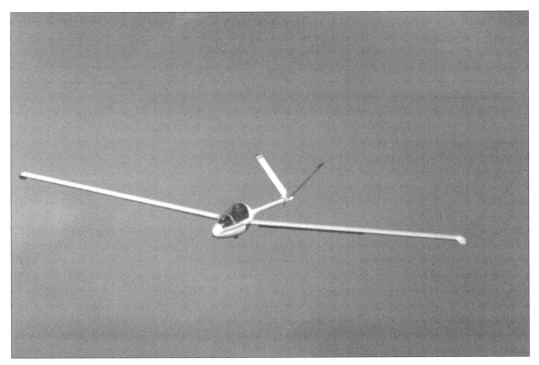

Landing the Veligdan Sailplane.

Begun in 1979, this high-performance, home-built sailplane was made by James Veligdan, a nuclear physicist at Brookhaven National Laboratory. Basically, Veligdan modified the design of a kit plane called the Monerai, enlarging the tail, lengthening the wing, and redesigning the cockpit and its enclosure.

The sailplane's fuselage is made of welded steel tubing covered with a fiberglass shell, and its wings and tail have aluminum spars and ribs with aluminum skins riveted on. The aircraft was designed for high-performance aerobatics (stressed to six Gs), and the wingtips can deflect as much as 48 inches under full load. The wingflaps can also deploy downward to 90 degrees for very steep descent paths. With a tow to approximately 5,000 feet, this sailplane can glide for about twenty-five miles. Today on Long Island soaring is a popular sport at both Brookhaven and Westhampton Beach Airports.

The aircraft on display, the only one ever built, was donated to the museum by Mr. James Veligdan.

Specifications

Wingspan: 42'
Length: 21'
Top Speed: 80 MPH
Weight: 330 lbs

Cassutt Special

HUNTINGTON, 1980

While employed as an airline pilot, Captain Tom Cassutt of Huntington designed and built in 1954 a small, single-seat racing aircraft known as the Cassutt Special No. 1. Based on Steve Wittman's "Buster" design, the Cassutt Special won the 1958 National Air Racing Championships. In 1959 Cassutt completed a smaller aircraft along the same lines, known as the Cassutt Special No. 2. Plans of both aircraft were made available to amateur constructors, and as a result, many Cassutt Specials have been built.

The Cassutt was a single-place, cantilevered mid-wing Formula One sport racer. It consisted of a simple-to-construct steel tube, wood, and fabric airplane stressed for aerobatics to 12 Gs. This very popular racing design is inexpensive yet offers high performance. The fuselage, engine mount, tail, and ailerons are constructed of steel tubing. The wing is all wood with the spar a simple flat piece of laminated spruce. The eighteen ribs are identical and of spruce truss construction. The wing skin is thin plywood or aluminum.

The aircraft on display is a one-of-a-kind two-seat version of the airplane, begun by Tom Cassutt and finished by members of the Experimental Aircraft Association, Chapter 594.

Donated by EAA Chapter 594.

Specifications

Wingspan: 14'11"
Length: 16'
Engine: 85 HP C-85 Continental
Top speed: 230 MPH
Weight: 526 lbs

A single-place Cassutt racer, ca. 1958.

Paramotor FX5

RONKONKOMA, 2000

Parachutes with power plants have opened up an entirely new field of sport aviation. Modern ram-air aerodynamic parachutes are flexible wing shapes with double surfaces and are kept inflated in flight by air flowing in from the front. They are steered by hand controls that twist the parachute. Today about five firms produce powered parachutes, the largest and most successful of which is the Paramotor Corporation of Oyster Bay. Paramotors are foot-launched; the pilot "wears" the engine and its shrouded propeller on his or her back. Launching and landing can be accomplished in ten feet or less. For takeoff, the pilot simply lays out the parachute behind him and the blast of air from the propeller inflates it while the pilot steps forward.

One of the smallest and safest aircraft in the world, the Paramotor does not require a license to fly. According to the manufacturer, full assembly takes less than five minutes, and no tools are required. Total cost is approximately $12,000. The Paramotor frame is made of aluminum alloy tubing, the canopy is ripstop nylon, and the fuel tank holds 1.25 gallons, giving the aircraft an average of one and a half hours in the air. Climb rate is 500 feet per minute, and maximum cruising altitude is 10,000 feet. The average person can learn to fly a Paramotor in two days.

The aircraft on display in one of over a thousand that have been built in Paramotor's plant in Ronkonkoma in both military and civilian versions. In fact, as of this writing, the Paramotor is the only flying machine in production on Long Island.

Donated by the Paramotor Corporation.

Landing an FX5.

Specifications

Span: 30'
Length: 15'
Engine: 27 HP Paramotor MZ34
Top speed: 50 MPH
Weight: 65 lbs

Grumman F-14A Tomcat

CALVERTON, 1971

The F-14 Tomcat, designed for fleet air defense and strike force protection, was the last in a long line of Grumman fighters for the U.S. Navy. Today 16 naval squadrons are still equipped with it. The Tomcat was the world's first operational air-superiority fighter with a variable-sweep wing, which can be automatically positioned for the best lift performance at various speeds. This versatility, and its AWG-9 weapons-control system, make the F-14 a true multimission fighter. Carrier-based, it has the sophisticated equipment to cope with high-speed, high-altitude aircraft and missile threats, yet is agile enough to win a dogfight. Its range is adequate to provide protection for today's far-reaching attack aircraft.

The Tomcat is manned by a crew of two; the pilot and the radar intercept officer, who operates the weapons-control system, the most capable ever carried by a fighter aircraft. It can detect hostile aircraft at ranges over 100 miles and has the ability to launch missiles at six different targets at once. It also has the ability to "see" and shoot down extremely small targets and to operate in a hostile electronic environment. The F-14 carries long-range Phoenix missiles, medium-range Sparrow missiles, and short-range Sidewinder missiles, as well as an M-161 Vulcan cannon.

In February 1969 the Navy selected Grumman to build this new fighter and the first one flew in late 1970. The first Tomcats were deployed with the fleet in 1974, and more recently F-14s have had numerous electronic and power-plant upgrades, most notably the F-14A+ and the F-14D. A total of 804 F-14s were built through 1994, all at Calverton, with subassembly in Bethpage.

The aircraft on display is the third F-14 built, and the oldest surviving. First flown in 1971, it remained in service until 1990, used primarily for flight testing of various improvements and determining flight characteristics under extreme conditions. The museum obtained it in 1995 and moved it by road from Calverton.

On loan from the National Museum of Naval Aviation.

Specifications

Wingspan: 38' swept, 64' unswept
Length: 61'11"
Top speed: 1,540 MPH
Engines: two Pratt & Whitney TF-30 20,000 lb-thrust
  turbofans
Weight: 38,000 lbs

A formation of three F-14 Tomcats from the aircraft carrier USS *Nimitz*.

Grumman A-6F Intruder

CALVERTON, 1987

The museum's Grumman A-6F Intruder.

The A-6 Intruder was conceived as a carrier-based low-level attack bomber equipped specifically to deliver nuclear or conventional weapons on targets completely obscured by weather or darkness. The Intruder possessed outstanding range and endurance and carried a heavier and more varied load of stores than any previous U.S. Naval attack aircraft. At one time it was operational with eighteen Navy and Marine Corps squadrons.

In continuous production from the late 1950s until 1994, the Intruder established a production longevity record that is unlikely to be equaled by any combat aircraft type manufactured in the West. Grumman was selected to develop the Intruder in 1957, and the first one flew in 1959. Production continued on the A model through 1969, with just under 500 being built. Its distinctly utilitarian appearance belied the fact that the A-6 was a sophisticated machine, effectively marrying computer technology with a sturdy airframe to produce a remarkably effective warplane.

The last production version of the Intruder was the E model, updated with a new radar, computer, and other improvements. Crewed by a pilot and bombardier/navigator (BN), the aircraft performed many missions, including close air support, interdiction, and deep strikes. It could detect, identify, track, and destroy tactical targets in any weather, day or night. The Intruder's five pylons could carry any of more than thirty types of bombs, rockets, missiles, or mines up to a total of 18,000 pounds. The BN operated the weapon delivery system, allowing the pilot to concentrate on tactical decisions. Unique displays showed targets and geographical features that ensured accurate weapon delivery despite night or bad weather. The A-6E incorporated Target Recognition Attack Multisensor (TRAM). TRAM provided television-type imagery of targets not detectable visually or by radar and was coupled to laser-guided weapons. Another version of the Intruder, the KA-6D tanker, refueled other aircraft in flight, while the EA-6B Prowler is still in service as an electronics warfare aircraft used to suppress enemy air defenses. A-6s were widely used, and were very effective, as attack aircraft in both the Vietnam and Persian Gulf wars. A total of 994 were built through 1993.

The aircraft on display is an F model, with additional ordnance pylons, more powerful engines, and new radars and digital avionics. It is one of three preproduction prototypes built at a cost of $220 million each in 1987. This A-6F was flown for a total of two and a half hours before the program was canceled.

On loan from the National Museum of Naval Aviation.

Specifications

Wingspan: 53'
Length: 54'9"
Engines: two General Electric 10,800 lb-thrust F-404s
Top speed: 640 MPH
Weight: 25, 740 lbs

Goddard A-Series Rocket

ROSWELL, NEW MEXICO, 1935 (replica)

Long Island's involvement with space flight can be traced back to its earliest days and the pioneering experiments in rocketry of Dr. Robert Goddard. In the early 1920s, working largely on his own in Massachusetts, Dr. Goddard developed and, in 1926, launched, the world's first liquid fuel rockets. A rather spectacular, noisy failed flight in 1929 caused his work to be banned in Massachusetts. Charles Lindbergh read a report of this flight and, impressed with the possibilities of the rocket, brought it to the attention of his friends, philanthropists Daniel and Harry Guggenheim of Sands Point.

Soon Dr. Goddard received $50,000 from Harry's private Guggenheim Fund—the first of several such grants that allowed him to continue his research at a time when those in government thought him a crackpot. With adequate funds, Goddard headed west to Roswell, New Mexico, where the climate and wide-open spaces were perfect for his work.

The Guggenheim Fund grants financed Goddard's work until 1940. During that time he developed a reliable liquid-fuel rocket engine, an efficient turbine fuel pump, a gyroscope-controlled steering system, and a parachute recovery system. Given the tools and technology of the time, his achievements were remarkable. In all, Goddard received no fewer than 214 patents covering virtually every aspect of liquid-fuel rockets. Thanks to Long Island funding, Goddard is the man behind every rocket that flies.

The rocket on display is a full-scale replica of a Goddard 1935 A series rocket. In the mid-1930s A series rockets flew successfully at speeds of over 600 MPH and to altitudes of about two miles.

Specifications

Length: 15'6"
Engine: Goddard 200 lb-thrust liquid-fuel
Top speed: 700 MPH
Weight: 85 lbs

Dr. Robert Goddard with an A-series rocket, 1935.

A Goddard rocket lifting off.

Republic JB-2/LTV-N2 "Buzz Bomb"

FARMINGDALE, 1945

Beginning in 1944 Germany began launching unmanned flying bombs, V-1s, at England from remote sites in France. Called "buzz bombs" by the British because of the loud noise they made, they flew at 5,000 feet and 400 MPH, and inflicted a fair amount of damage on several English cities. Of the 8,000 launched, half were shot down by fighters and anti-aircraft guns, but those that got through killed 5,500 people and destroyed 23,000 homes.

The U.S. Army was interested in starting a missile program, so a captured unexploded V-1 was sent to Wright Field for study. In September 1944 Republic Aviation of Farmingdale was awarded a contract to build exact duplicates of these V-1s for use by the Army. In exactly two months' time, the first operational versions, now known as JB-2s (Jet Bomb Model 2), rolled off Republic's assembly lines. A number of JB-2s were diverted to the Navy and designated as LTV-N2 "Loons." These flying bombs were used in a pioneering program to launch missiles off ships and submarines.

In all, some 1,200 JB-2s were built by Republic and several subcontractors. Built entirely of steel and powered by Ford Pulsejet engines, 800 of these missiles were eventually launched from bases in Florida and New Mexico. Republic JB-2s were the first U.S. guided missiles to be mass-produced, as well as the first to be launched from submarines. Each able to carry almost a ton of high explosives, they were set for use in the planned invasion of Japan when World War II ended.

Although a crude and inaccurate missile by modern standards, the buzz bomb can be considered a direct ancestor of today's cruise missiles.

On loan from the U.S. Navy.

Specifications

Wingspan: 17'4"
Length: 25'4"
Engine: Ford 770 lb-thrust Pulsejet
Top speed: 420 MPH
Weight: 4,800 lbs

A "buzz bomb" in launching position aboard ship.

Fairchild Petrel

WYANDANCH, 1951

In the late 1940s the Fairchild Guided Missiles Division was established in Wyandanch, in central Long Island, for the development of new types of military missiles. Among its earliest products was the Petrel, a revolutionary new missile that became operational in the early 1950s. The Petrel was an air-launched missile, usually carried by a Lockheed Neptune, designed for use against both surface ships and submarines. It essentially consisted of an Mk-13 torpedo fitted to a jet-powered airframe. The torpedo would shed the airframe at a predetermined range and enter the water as a conventional homing torpedo.

The Petrel provided to long-range patrol aircraft an all-weather offensive capability against enemy ships and submarines that was able to remain beyond the effective range of those ships' defensive armament. It was the most complex Navy missile of its time. After the Petrel, Fairchild produced for the Navy the Lark, a rocket-propelled surface-to-air missile, in quantity.

On loan from the National Air and Space Museum.

Specifications

Wingspan: 13'
Length: 24'
Top speed: 500 MPH
Engine: Fairchild J-44 1,000 lb-thrust turbojet
Weight: 3,800 lbs

A Petrel under the wing of a PV-2 patrol plane, 1954.

Grumman XSSM-N-6 Rigel

BETHPAGE, 1952

A Rigel lifts off.

Grumman was awarded the contract to build the large Rigel ship-to-surface missile in 1946. Rigel was the earliest large submarine-launched shore-bombardment nuclear missile, a predecessor of the Regulus, Polaris, and Poseidon missiles. Although Rigel itself did not become operational and was canceled after Grumman worked on its development from 1946 to 1953, much was learned from work in the submarine and launching phase that was useful for the development of later missiles. Rigel was Grumman's first missile project and led the company to expand its missile and spacecraft interests. It was also considered an early cruise missile and may have helped influence early strategic thinking along these lines.

Rigel was the first successful U.S. "ramjet" missile, the first Mach 2 vehicle, and Grumman's first weapons system. Rigel had a solid-fuel first stage that boosted the missile to Mach 1 (the speed of sound), at which speed the ramjet second stage kicked in and boosted the speed to Mach 2. Rigel had a 400-mile range at altitudes up to 50,000 feet. Thirteen Rigels were successfully launched from Point Mugu, California, between 1950 and 1953.

The Rigel on display is the only surviving example of this type of missile.

On loan from the National Air and Space Museum.

Specifications

Length: 41'2"
Wingspan: 11'10"
Engine: Grumman/Marquardt 20,000 lb-thrust Ramjet
Top speed: 1,500 MPH
Weight: 6,200 lbs

Republic Terrapin

FARMINGDALE, 1956 (replica)

Republic's first nonmilitary missile was the Terrapin, manufactured in the 1950s as a high-altitude research rocket. It was developed in conjunction with the University of Maryland and named after the school's mascot, a turtle. It was a lightweight, low-cost, high-performance vehicle, and on its first firing, in July 1956 from Wallops Island, Virginia, it raced eighty miles into space at a speed of 3,800 MPH, sending back scientific data by radio. A solid-propellant rocket motor fired Terrapin, which reached an altitude of 10,000 feet in six seconds at 1,900 MPH. The first stage of the rocket then separated from the second stage, which coasted another 30,000 feet, at which point the second-stage motor shot Terrapin to 100,000 feet at Mach 5.8. The rocket then coasted the rest of the way to peak altitude. Carrying six pounds of scientific instruments, the missile took only 5.6 minutes to complete its one-way missions.

Both the Terrapin and its collapsible, zero-length launcher could be transported in a standard-size station wagon, and a crew of three could easily set it up and fire it. Terrapins were also launched from ships off the Virginia coast. One important use of these missiles was to obtain data that could be analyzed to formulate an integrated picture of the earth's upper atmosphere. It thus gathered the information about cosmic rays and upper air temperatures which was necessary in order to properly plan future spacecraft. Republic produced a small quantity of Terrapins through 1957. It was the only Long Island-built scientific research rocket.

No original Terrapins survive. The full-scale replica on display was built from original plans.

A Terrapin being launched.

Specifications

Length: 15'
Diameter: 6"
Engines: two, solid propellant
Top speed: 3,800 MPH
Weight: 225 lbs

Convair/Sperry SAM-N-7 Terrier

LAKE SUCCESS AND POMONA, CALIFORNIA, 1956

The first operational surface-to-air missile of the U.S. Navy, Terrier was an offshoot of the Bumblebee ramjet program begun in 1945 by Johns Hopkins University. It was first fired from a ship in 1951, went into full production in 1952 and became operational in 1956. It remained in Navy service as an air defense missile into the mid 1960s. The guidance systems for these missiles were produced by the Sperry Gyroscope Corporation on Long Island.

A versatile weapon, the Terrier could be fired day or night and in all weather conditions. The system was completely automatic. Missiles were selected automatically from a magazine and loaded onto the launcher, which was automatically trained, elevated, and fired. The whole operation took about 30 seconds. A shipboard AN-55 surface-acquisition radar, also built on Long Island by Sperry, guided each two-stage missile to its target.

On loan from the U.S. Navy.

Specifications

Length: 27'
Wingspan: 42"
Engines: two Allegany Ballistics,
    solid-propellant
Top speed: 1,875 MPH
Weight: 3,200 lbs

Terrier missiles aboard a U.S. Navy destroyer.

67

Douglas Nike Hercules Missile

SANTA MONICA, CALIFORNIA, 1960

In the 1950s, in order to counter the threat of Soviet missiles and bombers, antiaircraft missile sites were set up all around New York City to protect the metropolitan area. The six Long Island sites were at Rocky Point, Brookville, Lloyd Neck, Farmingdale, Long Beach, and Rockaway. Nike Ajax missiles were installed at first, succeeded later by Nike Hercules missiles equipped with nuclear warheads. Part of a medium- and high-level air defense system, such missiles were placed in fixed sites to defend many large American cities from Soviet air attacks. Each site had its own acquisition and tracking radar as well as self-sufficient launch control.

The Nike Hercules missile, introduced in 1958, was the second land-based, combat ready surface-to-air guided missile to become an integral part of America's air defense system at the height of the Cold War in the 1950s and 60s. Successor to the Nike Ajax, it was part of a system, built by Sperry, that electronically acquired a target and launched a missile to destroy it. It could engage either single planes, formations of aircraft or incoming intercontinental ballistic missiles. It was equipped with a nuclear warhead, whose detonation would destroy its target even without a direct hit. Launched by remote control, the Hercules received its initial burst of speed from a cluster of four solid-propellant boosters and was accelerated by a solid-fuel sustainer. The dart-shaped second stage had fins with movable control surfaces in order to steer the missile to its target.

The nuclear-equipped Nike missiles traveled at Mach 3.65 with a range of eighty miles. The sites were all decommissioned around 1972.

Donated by the U.S. Army.

Specifications

Length: 41'
Diameter: 2'8"
Engines: five Thiokol 2,600 lb-thrust solid-fuel
Top speed: 4,200 MPH
Weight: 12,050 lbs

A Nike Hercules on its launchpad.

A Nike Hercules base on the Atlantic Ocean at Rockaway Beach, ca. 1962.

Lockheed/Sperry A-2 Polaris

LAKE SUCCESS AND SUNNYVALE, CALIFORNIA, 1964

Perfection of this missile represented one of the greatest achievements in missile engineering up to that time. Pentagon planners had decided to place missiles on submarines as a deterrent to conflict, since their precise position would always be difficult for an enemy to locate. The problem presented to Lockheed and its subcontractors in 1956 was to produce a nuclear missile small enough to be carried in quantity by a submarine and capable of underwater launching. They succeeded so well that by 1962 eight submarines, each carrying 16 Polaris missiles, had been commissioned. Eventually, there were 41 Polaris submarines.

Operationally, Polaris was forced out of its vertical storage tube in the submarine by compressed air, and its first-stage rocket motor fired as soon as it broke clear of the surface. The missile had a range of 2,800 miles. Steering was accomplished by tilting the nozzles of the rocket motor.

The Sperry Corporation of Lake Success designed and built the complex inertial guidance system used in the missile as well as the submarine navigation system that was used to establish the latitude and longitude of the ship precisely, thus ensuring an accurate trajectory for any missile fired from it. The Polaris missile was replaced by the Poseidon in 1982, and later by the Trident. Sperry played a major role in both of these programs.

Specifications

Length: 31'
Diameter: 4'6"
Engines: Two Aerojet solid-propellant
Top speed: 6,600 MPH
Weight: 35,700

A test launch of an A-2 Polaris.

Maxson AQM-37A Target Missile

GREAT RIVER, 1972

This supersonic target missile was used to simulate enemy missile threats and for air-to-air and surface-to-air missile evaluation and training exercises. It was equipped to provide active or passive radar augmentation for simulated enemy systems, either aircraft or missiles, and a chemical flare was available for infrared augmentation. Two miss-distance indication systems were also available.

The target missile was normally air-launched, but it did have surface launch capability, from shipboard or land-based launcher systems. The target's universal launch capability and high performance uniquely suited it to a number of tactical and support missions. The target utilized a liquid bipropellant rocket engine. The engine consisted of a booster and sustain-er thrust chamber, a selector valve for propellant flow control, fuel and oxidizer, and nitrogen tankage. The AQM-37A was originally produced by the Beech Aircraft Corporation with Maxson Electronics on Long Island as a second supplier.

Specifications

Length: 14'2"
Width: 13"
Engine: Rocketdyne 630 lb-thrust
Top speed: 1,700 MPH
Weight: 565 lbs

An AQM-37A mounted on a standard under-wing pylon.

Maxson AGM-12B and AGM-12C Bullpups

GREAT RIVER, 1970

A crew attaches a Bullpup to a wing.

The Bullpup was an air-to-surface missile designed in the 1960s for use against ground targets that required pinpoint accuracy in the delivery of a conventional warhead. It was conceived by the U.S. Navy as a simple weapon built around a standard 250-pound bomb powered by a Navy-developed solid-propellant rocket motor.

Production of the Bullpup was initially undertaken by the Martin-Marietta Corporation. The Maxson Electronics Corporation of Great River, Long Island was contracted as a second supplier. Maxson eventually assumed all production of models AGM-12B, carrying a standard 250-pound high-explosive warhead, and the larger AGM-12C, carrying either 1,000 pounds of conventional explosives or a nuclear warhead.

Guidance for the AGM-12B, one of the first "smart bombs," was visual. The pilot would locate the target, launch the missile, and guide it to the target by means of a control stick connected to a radio transmitter—a method similar to that used in operating a radio-controlled model aircraft. To assist the pilot in maintaining visual contact with the missile, two high density flares were placed on the sides of the motor exhaust.

Bullpups were extensively used during the latter part of the Vietnam War, launched from F-105D Thunderchiefs and F4 Phantoms. Because of a lack of new contracts, Maxson was forced to close in the mid-1970s.

Specifications

AGM-12B	AGM-12C
Length: 10'6"	Length: 13'4"
Diameter: 1'	Diameter: 1'5"
Engine: Thiokol LR 58	Engine: Thiokol 1,100 lb-thrust LR 68
Top speed: 1,400 MPH	Top speed: 1,400 MPH
Weight: 570 lbs	Weight: 1,790 lbs

Sputnik Satellite

SOVIET UNION, 1957 (replica)

On October 4, 1957, the Soviet Union shocked the world and successfully placed the world's first artificial satellite, named Sputnik, into orbit around the earth. Sputnik was several times heavier than the largest satellites then being prepared for launching as part of Project Vanguard, America's satellite program. Sputnik, meaning "traveler" in Russian, had two radio transmitters aboard that broadcast the famous "beep-beep-beep" signaling the start of the space age. These radio signals were first detected in the United States by the RCA radio communications station at Riverhead.

Scientific information obtained from Sputnik came primarily from observations of its orbit and the rate at which the orbit decayed. Even so, the significance of Sputnik can hardly be overestimated. Reaction to the technological accomplishment was dramatic and disturbing to many in America. To people in many countries, it appeared to show the superiority of the Soviet system. The reaction to Sputnik led to several important events in the United States. Among these were the establishment of the National Aeronautics and Space Administration (NASA) and the enactment by Congress of the National Defense Education Act of 1958, which called for stricter standards for math and science in public schools. In all probability the United States could have placed a satellite in orbit prior to the Soviets, but the project was given very low priority by the Eisenhower Administration. Sputnik's most important legacy was that it ignited the Cold War "space race" which culminated in 1969 with America's landing on the moon.

This full-scale replica of Sputnik was made in the former Soviet Union and was given to the people of Nassau County by the government of the Soviet Union in 1987.

Specifications

Diameter: 23"
Weight: 184 lbs

An artist's rendering of Sputnik in space.

Grumman Molab

In order to gain insight into the problems of driving a vehicle on the moon, in the early 1960s Grumman built with its own funds the Mobile Lunar Laboratory (Molab). This vehicle would have provided two exploring astronauts a 250-mile range in a pressurized environment complete with its own laboratory for up to thirty days. Under a NASA contract Grumman used this vehicle to investigate the driving characteristics of a lunar roving vehicle over a simulated lunar surface at their Calverton plant. The forward section contained the controls, two seats, beds, work areas, communications equipment, and a laboratory. The rear section contained batteries to drive the individual electric motors for each wheel.

Molab was designed for an unmanned landing on the Lunar surface, to be followed by a manned Lunar Module landing nearby. The crew would then drive the Molab off a modified LM descent stage. Although never used on the moon, Molab gathered valuable information on vehicle performance on a simulated lunar surface. The unusual Grumman wheel design (Metalastic) acted as a shock absorber and took on an elliptical shape under load to give a larger "footprint." It is still under active consideration for use on a future Mars roving vehicle.

Donated by the Grumman Aerospace Corporation.

Specifications

Length: 31'
Width: 9'
Engine: four reversible electric motors
Top speed: 15 MPH

Molab on simulated lunar surface.

Rockwell Command Module

DOWNEY, CALIFORNIA, 1965

The Command Module (CM) was the control center for the Apollo spacecraft and provided the living and working quarters for the three-man crew for the entire lunar flight, except for the period when two crewmen were traveling in the Lunar Module between lunar orbit and the lunar surface. The Command Module consisted of the inner crew compartment (pressure vessel), surrounded by a stainless steel honeycomb and an outer heat shield, thickest on the rear, made of heat-dissipating material that burned away during the 25,000-MPH re-entry into the earth's atmosphere. Astronauts entered the docked Lunar Module through the hatch in the nose, while the hatch on the side provided entry and exit to the Command Module. Parachutes for landing were stored in the Command Module's nose, for deployment following re-entry. The parachutes seen here were flown to the Moon and back on Apollo 15. The Command Module was the only part of the 364-foot-tall Saturn rocket that returned to Earth.

In order to test the launch escape system for the Apollo Command Module, NASA developed the fin-stabilized, solid-propellant, 88-foot tall Little Joe II rocket. This rocket would be able to propel a full-sized Apollo Command Module to velocities as great as those in the critical portions of the Saturn V trajectory, at altitudes of 30 miles. Before manned Apollo flights began in 1967, one last abort qualification test was made with the Little Joe II. On January 20, 1966, Apollo Test Mission 004 was launched with this very CM, number 002, headed toward an altitude of 24 miles. For this test, the launch vehicle started to tumble, as planned, and the CM launch escape system sensed trouble and fired its abort rocket, carrying the CM away from impending disaster. The CM was recovered normally by parachute after a hard landing in the desert. All went well, the test successfully proved that the CM launch escape system and earth landing systems could protect the astronauts in either emergency or normal operations. This was the last flight before the Apollo 1 fire.

Long Island also had a very important connection to the development of the Command Module. In 1965, before the it was flown with men in it, Republic Aviation built a sub-scale prototype CM called the Project Fire spacecraft. Two successful flights with this vehicle proved that the CM would be stable during re-entry and that the heat shield would work at lunar return speeds.

On loan from the National Air and Space Museum.

The museum's Rockwell Command Module prior to launch, 1966.

Specifications

Height: 10'7"
Diameter: 12'10"
Re-entry speed: 25,000 MPH
Weight: 12, 235 lbs

Another Rockwell Command Module, photographed in space from the Lunar Module *Challenger*.

Grumman Lunar Module Simulator

BETHPAGE AND BINGHAMTON, NEW YORK, 1968

This Lunar Module (LM) Mission Simulator, a large, complex device, was in operation at the Kennedy Space Center between 1968 and 1972. It was used by all the Apollo astronauts before their missions to train for landing on the moon. Only one was built, and, remarkably, it survived in good condition. This is a very significant artifact, one of the few key pieces remaining from the Apollo program.

The device consists of a simulator cabin (LM ascent stage with complete original interior), four large rear projectors and screens mounted outside the windows, an operator's console, tape-drive computers, and a simulated lunar surface model and camera. Instructors at the console could introduce malfunctions into the simulated mission the astronauts were running inside. Cameras, filming a model of the lunar surface, projected the image in front of the LM windows so the astronauts would feel as if they were actually maneuvering for a landing on the Moon. Astronauts would even sleep overnight inside this device in preparation for three-day stays on the moon.

The Lunar Module Simulator was produced by Link in conjunction with the Grumman Aircraft Corporation.

On loan from the National Air and Space Museum.

Neal Armstrong, commander of Apollo 11, practices for his historic landing on the moon
in the Lunar Module Simulator at the Kennedy Space Center, 1969.

Grumman Lunar Module LM-13

BETHPAGE, 1972

In November 1962 the Grumman Corporation won the competition to build the Project Apollo Lunar Module (LM). It was the first spaceship designed to take humans from one world to another. As such, it came to be regarded as the most historically important vehicle ever built on Long Island. Grumman's original design evolved through several configurations over the years—and kept on changing through each successive mission. As the complexity of the task increased, so did the number of people working on it. At one point 9,000 employees of Grumman were assigned to the Lunar Module project.

Unlike aircraft, the LMs were not produced on an assembly line—every one was handmade, one at a time. Each LM consisted of an ascent stage and a descent stage, with both stages functioning as a single unit after separation from the Command Module (CM) through descent, landing, and stay on the lunar surface. The descent stage then served as the launch platform from which the ascent stage lifted off the moon. Interstage fittings were severed by explosives, so that the ascent stage then operated as an independent spacecraft during liftoff, ascent, rendezvous, and docking with the Command Module in lunar orbit. Thermal and micrometeoroid shields also covered the descent stage. This shield, of aluminized Mylar, gave the craft a fragile, almost flimsy appearance. The ascent stage was the control center of the LM, with positions for two astronauts. It contained the systems required for navigation, control, communications, life support, electrical power, and propulsion. The descent stage, the unmanned portion of the LM, carried the scientific equipment and experiments that were used on the lunar surface, as well as the descent propulsion system.

The Lunar Module was the first true spacecraft, performing its mission only in the vacuum of space. Because of this, it could be designed to be purely functional, without streamlining—no aerodynamic qualities were necessary.

On July 20, 1969, when Neil Armstrong and Edwin Aldrin became the first human beings in history to walk on another world, a Grumman Lunar Module, the LM-5 *Eagle*, got them there. In all, six manned LMs successfully landed twelve men on the Moon between 1969 and 1972. A seventh, on the Apollo 13 mission, served as a lifeboat for its crew

The Lunar Module on display, LM-13, was slated for the Apollo 19 mission, which was ultimately canceled. The museum also has on exhibit the LTA-1, the first fully functional LM, built for testing on Earth. It is displayed without skin and legs, as it appeared while under construction at Grumman.

The LTA is on loan from, and the LM was donated by, the National Air and Space Museum.

Specifications

Height: 22'9"
Width: 31'
Engines:
   ascent: Rocketdyne 3,500 lb-thrust
   descent: TRW, 9,870 lb-thrust
   reaction control: 16 Marquardt thrusters (100 lb-thrust)
Top speed: 17,500 MPH
Weight: 8,600 lbs

The Apollo 15 Lunar Module on the moon, 1971.

A Lunar Module under construction at Grumman's "clean room," Bethpage, 1970.

Microcraft/GASL X-43

RONKONKOMA AND TULLAHOMA, TENNESSEEE, 2000 (replica)

The X-43 aerospace plane, designed and partially built on Long Island, is equipped with the world's first hypersonic scramjet engine.

This is the future of flight: the next generation of space-craft, and aircraft, will be fully reusable single-stage-to-orbit aerospace planes that take off and land on runways. Future airliners built along these lines will be able to fly passengers between New York and Tokyo in about an hour. They will be powered by revolutionary new types of engine such as the Long Island-built General Applied Sciences Laboratories (GASL) hypersonic scramjet.

The first craft ever built to test such an engine is the X-43, a NASA experimental vehicle. It is the fastest aircraft ever built. Three X-43s were test-flown in 2001, at speeds up to Mach 10, or ten times the speed of sound. Each was launched atop a Pegasus rocket and separated at 100,000 feet over the Pacific Ocean before flying under its own power for a thousand miles. (These flights were unmanned, and none of the planes was recovered.)

Unlike a rocket, which must carry its own oxygen for combustion, an air-breathing craft like the X-43 scoops air from the atmosphere. Thus future aerospace planes, by eliminating the weight of the heavy oxygen tanks, will be able to carry heavier loads than rockets.

"Scramjet" engines operate only at "hypersonic" speeds above Mach 5. The X-43's GASL engine, burning hydrogen fuel, was the first to power an aircraft to such speeds. Its new propulsion system compressed air for the engine by using the forward speed of the aircraft; thus no compressor blades were required. The X-43's body itself was used to form part of the engine, with the fore section serving as an intake and the aft section as the exhaust nozzle.

The vehicle on exhibit is a full-scale replica built by museum volunteers.

Specifications

Wingspan: 5'
Length: 12'
Top speed: 7,300 MPH
Engine: GASL Hypersonic Scramjet
Weight: 2,200 lbs

The X-43 soars at supersonic speed.

Boeing 707 (nose section)

SEATTLE, WASHINGTON, 1961

El Al's record-breaking Boeing 707, from which the museum's nose cone was salvaged.

The Boeing 707 represented a turning point in transportation history; its introduction marked the true beginning of a new age in travel. The 707 changed the way people thought about travel, and it changed the aircraft industry. Boeing had never enjoyed real commercial success with its previous airliners, but the 707 gave birth to a "family" of transports that have since dominated the global airliner market.

Funded with $16 million of Boeing's own funds, the new four-engine, 600-MPH, 160-seat jet transport first flew on July 15, 1954. First ordered by Pan American in 1955, it went into transatlantic service between New York and London in 1958. The almost 950 Boeing 707s sold set a new standard for travelers and Boeing became a household word in the exciting new jet era.

The 707 nose section on display is from the aircraft designated 4X-ATA, the first jet operated by El Al Israel Airlines. It was delivered in May 1961 and had the honor of establishing two world records. On June 15, 1961, during the return (eastbound) portion of its scheduled round trip between Tel Aviv and New York, 4X-ATA flew 5,760 miles nonstop—a new distance record for a scheduled commercial flight. Accomplished in 9 hours, 33 minutes, this flight also set the speed record for a commercial flight from New York to Tel Aviv. 4X-ATA served for 23 years, retiring in 1984. In all, it carried over two million passengers more than 36 million miles, equivalent to circling the world 1,450 times, without incident.

Donated by El Al Israel Airlines.

Specifications

Wingspan: 145'
Length: 152'
Engines: four Pratt & Whitney JT3P 11,000 lb-thrust turbojets
Top speed: 630 MPH
Weight: 150,000 lbs

The Boeing 707 nose section being unloaded at the museum.

A Lunar Module cockpit trainer.

The Cradle of Aviation Museum is also fortunate to have gathered an excellent collection of aircraft cockpits relevent to the museum's mission. These cockpit sections are not only rare and difficult to obtain, they also afford the visitor a unique opportunity to see inside a historic aircraft—a view not normally obtainable. The following cockpit sections are usually on exhibit at the museum. As with the aircraft, all have undergone restoration by the museum's skilled volunteer staff.

The museum's A-10 nose section, photographed as the plane was broken up.

An F-14 nose section during restoration.

DOUGLAS C-47

An actual nose section from the famous DC-3, repainted in the markings of a Long Islander's World War II C-47 transport.

GRUMMAN S2F

A simulator for the 1950s-60s Tracker anti-submarine aircraft.

REPUBLIC F-105D

An original simulator for the Vietnam-era Thunderchief bomber, possibly the only one left.

REPUBLIC A-10A

A nose section from an actual A-10 Thunderbolt II, repainted as a Gulf War attack aircraft.

GRUMMAN LUNAR MODULE

An engineering trainer, identical to the original, used at Grumman in the development of the Lunar Module. This cockpit has been modified into an interactive exhibit.

GRUMMAN E-2C

A nose section removed from a Hawkeye early warning aircraft, reworked into a carrier landing simulator.

GRUMMAN F-14A

An actual Tomcat fighter cockpit section, removed from an early F-14—possibly the only one on exhibit anywhere.

CONVAIR 240

The cockpit section from an original Convair airliner, a type commonly seen at LaGuardia and Idlewild (Kennedy) airports in the late 1940s and early 1950s. Visitors can try this one out!

GRUMMAN A-6

This was a simulator for Grumman's historic Intruder bomber from the Vietnam and Gulf Wars. It has been modified for visitors to sit in.

A C-47 nose section in the markings of the "Long Island Duck."

A Convair 240 nose section.

Index